The Evolution of the Israeli Third Sector: A Conceptual and Empirical Analysis

Voluntaristics Review

Editor-in-Chief

David Horton Smith (*Boston College, USA*)

Deputy Editors

John McNutt (*University of Delaware, USA*)
Richard Steinberg (*Indiana University-Purdue University at Indianapolis, USA*)
Lili Wang (*Arizona State University, USA / China*)

Associate Editors

Samir Abu-Rumman (*Global Center for Philanthropy Studies, Kuwait / Jordan*)
Abdullah Al-Khalifa (*National Center for Social Studies, Saudi Arabia*)
Aries Arugay (*University of the Philippines at Diliman, Philippines*)
Doug Baer (*University of Victoria, Canada*)
René Bekkers (*VU University Amsterdam, Netherlands*)
Oonagh B. Breen (*University College Dublin, Ireland*)
Grace Chikoto (*University of Wisconsin-Milwaukee, USA*)
Vincent Chua (*National University of Singapore, Singapore*)
Ram A. Cnaan (*University of Pennsylvania, USA / Israel*)
Carolyn Cordery (*Victoria University of Wellington, New Zealand, & Aston University, UK*)
Noshir Dadrawala (*Centre for Advancement of Philanthropy, India*)
Bronwen Dalton (*University of Technology Sydney, Australia*)
Thomas Davies (*City, University of London, UK*)
Justin Davis-Smith (*City, University of London, UK*)
Angela Ellis-Paine (*University of Birmingham, UK*)
Sherine El-Taraboulsi (*University of Oxford, UK / Egypt*)
Jurgen Grotz (*University of East Anglia, UK / Germany*)
Chao Guo (*University of Pennsylvania, USA / China*)
Adam Habib (*University of the Witwatersrand, South Africa*)
Mark Hager (*Arizona State University, USA*)
Debbie Haski-Leventhal (*Macquarie University, Australia / Israel*)
Steinunn Hrafnsdottir (*University of Iceland, Iceland*)
Lev Jakobson (*National Research University Higher School of Economics, Russian Federation*)
Emma Juaneda-Ayensa (*La Rioja University, Spain*)
Chulhee Kang (*Yonsei University, South Korea*)
Helena Kuvikova (*Matej Bel University, Slovakia*)
Benjamin Lough (*University of Illinois, USA*)
Jacob Mwathi Mati (*University of the South Pacific at Laucala, Fiji / Kenya*)

Myles McGregor-Lowndes (*Queensland University of Technology, Australia*)
Irina Mersianova (*National Research University Higher School of Economics, Russian Federation*)
Carl Milofsky (*Bucknell University, USA*)
Alisa Moldavanova (*Wayne State University, USA / Ukraine*)
Andrew Morris (*Union College, USA*)
Bhekinkosi Moyo (*Southern Africa Trust, South Africa*)
Hanna Nel (*University of Johannesburg, South Africa*)
Rebecca Nesbit (*University of Georgia, USA*)
Ebenezer Obadare (*University of Kansas, USA / Nigeria*)
Tomofumi Oka (*Sophia University, Japan*)
Aya Okada (*Kanazawa University, Japan*)
Jennie Onyx (*University of Technology Sydney, Australia*)
Anne B. Pessi (*University of Helsinki, Finland*)
Ruman Petrov (*New Bulgarian University, Bulgaria*)
Cristian Pliscoff (*University of Chile, Chile*)
Tereza Pospisilova (*Charles University, Czech Republic*)
Lionel Prouteau (*Université de Nantes, France*)
Jack Quarter (*University of Toronto, Canada*)
Colin Rochester (*Birkbeck University, UK*)
Krishna Roka (*University of Wisconsin-Stevens Point, USA / Nepal*)
Boguslawa Sardinha (*Instituto Politécnico de Setúbal, Portugal*)
Gregory D. Saxton (*SUNY, University of Buffalo, USA*)
Per Selle (*University of Bergen, Norway*)
Robert A. Stebbins (*University of Calgary, Canada / USA*)
Hironori Tarumi (*Hokkai-Gakuen University, Japan*)
Marilyn Taylor (*University of the West of England, UK*)
Lars Torpe (*Aalborg University, Denmark*)
Stijn Van Puyvelde (*Vrije Universiteit Brussel, Belgium*)
Jon Van Til (*Rutgers University-Camden, USA*)
Ming Wang (*Tsinghua University, China*)
Na Wei (*Renmin University, China*)
Pamala Wiepking (*Erasmus University, Netherlands*)
Fengshi Wu (*Nanyang Technological University, Singapore / China*)
Xinye Wu (*East China University of Political Science and Law, China*)
Ruijun Yuan (*Peking University, China*)
Chao Zhang (*Soo Chow University, China*)
Zhibin Zhang (*Flinders University, Australia / China*)
Jiangang Zhu (*Sun Yat-sen University, China*)
Annette Zimmer (*University of Münster, Germany*)

Volumes published in this Brill Research Perspectives title are listed at *brill.com/vrbr*

The Evolution of the Israeli Third Sector: A Conceptual and Empirical Analysis

By

Rachel Calipha
Benjamin Gidron

BRILL

LEIDEN | BOSTON

This paperback book edition is simultaneously published as issue 5.4 (2020) of *Voluntaristics Review*, DOI: 10.1163/24054933-12340034

ICSERA is a global infrastructure organization, research-information institute, and umbrella association for voluntaristics (nonprofit, third sector) researcher associations (www.icsera.org). A Florida-based, IRS-501(c) (3) nonprofit 2010+, the International Council of Voluntarism, Civil Society, and Social Economy Researcher Associations officially sponsors *Voluntaristics Review* and the *Palgrave Handbook of Volunteering, Civic Participation, and Nonprofit Associations.*

Library of Congress Control Number: 2021933907

Typeface for the Latin, Greek, and Cyrillic scripts: "Brill". See and download: brill.com/brill-typeface.

ISBN 978-90-04-46172-7 (paperback)
ISBN 978-90-04-46173-4 (e-book)

Copyright 2021 by Rachel Calipha and Benjamin Gidron. Published by Koninklijke Brill NV, Leiden, The Netherlands.
Koninklijke Brill NV incorporates the imprints Brill, Brill Hes & De Graaf, Brill Nijhoff, Brill Rodopi, Brill Sense, Hotei Publishing, mentis Verlag, Verlag Ferdinand Schöningh and Wilhelm Fink Verlag.
Koninklijke Brill NV reserves the right to protect this publication against unauthorized use. Requests for re-use and/or translations must be addressed to Koninklijke Brill NV via brill.com or copyright.com.

This book is printed on acid-free paper and produced in a sustainable manner.

Contents

The Evolution of the Israeli Third Sector: A Conceptual and Empirical Analysis   1

      Rachel Calipha and Benjamin Gidron

    Abstract   1

    Keywords   2

    Editor's Introduction to VR 5.4: Voluntaristics as the Larger Context of the Current *VR* Issue on Nonprofit/Third Sector Research in Israel   2

1   Introduction   5

2   Introduction to the Israeli Third Sector: A Theoretical Analysis   6

3   The Introduction of the Third Sector *Concept* in Israel   12

    3.1   *The Early Beginnings: The 1970s and 1980s*   12

    3.2   *The Conferences that Changed the Picture*   14

    3.3   *The Johns Hopkins Project*   14

4   Legal and Economic Characteristics of the Israeli Third Sector   15

    4.1   *The Legal Dimension*   15

    4.2   *The Economic Dimension*   17

        4.2.1   Current Economic Data   17

        4.2.2   Employees and Volunteers   18

        4.2.3   Characteristics of Workforce   19

5   Civil Society and Social Movements—The Associational Perspective   20

    5.1   *The Associational Perspective: Organizations of the Civil Society in Israel*   20

    5.2   *Sources of Funding*   21

    5.3   *Social Movements*   22

6   Policy Development towards the Third Sector   23

    6.1   *Lack of Recognition*   24

    6.2   *The Galnoor Committee*   25

    6.3   *The Round Tables Project*   27

    6.4   *The Aridor Committee*   27

    6.5   *The Lebanon War*   28

    6.6   *In the Aftermath of the 2008 Economic Crisis*   30

7   Philanthropy   30

    7.1   *Donations: Current Data*   33

8   Philanthropy and Civil Society in the Arab-Palestinian Society   33

9   Social Entrepreneurship and Social Enterprises   34

10   Research, Databases, Journals, and Education Centers   35

11   Conclusions   36

Appendix I: The Economic Dimension   38
Appendix II: Civil Society and Social Movements   39
(a)   *Supports under Article 3A*   39
(b)   *Grants from Social Security Funds*   41
(c)   *Grants from a Foreign Political Entity*   41
(d)   *Social Movement Organizations*   43
Appendix III: Philanthropy   45
(a)   *Israel Donations*   45
(b)   *Donations from Abroad*   46
(c)   *Large Donations from Israel*   48
(d)   *Large Donations from Abroad*   49
(e)   *Tax Credit Certificate for Donation*   49
(f)   *Large Donations by Size*   50
Appendix IV: Arab-Palestinians in Israel Civil Society   53
(a)   *Government Funding*   53
(b)   *Employees and Volunteers*   53
Appendix V: Research Centers, Databases, Education Programs, and
Journals   54
(a)   *Research Centers*   54
　　　(i)　　The Israeli Center for Third Sector Research (ICTR) at
　　　　　　Ben-Gurion University of the Negev   54
　　　(ii)　 The Center for the Study of Civil Society and Philanthropy
　　　　　　in Israel   55
　　　(iii)　Taub Center for Social Policy Studies in Israel at Tel Aviv
　　　　　　University   56
　　　(iv)　 The Walter Lebach Institute for Jewish-Arab Coexistence
　　　　　　through Education   56
　　　(v)　　The Van Leer Jerusalem Institute   57
　　　(vi)　 The Knesset Research and Information Center (RIC)   57
　　　(vii)　The Israel Democracy Institute (IDI)   57
　　　(viii)　JDC Institute for Leadership and Governance   57
(b)   *Databases*   58
　　　(i)　　The National Bureau of Statistics (NBS)   58
　　　(ii)　 GuideStar   58
　　　(iii)　Social Map   58
　　　(iv)　 Ruach Tova   58
　　　(v)　　Midot   59
(c)   *Education Programs*   59

CONTENTS   IX

(d) *Journals*   59
    (i)   Civil Society and The Third Sector in Israel   59
    (ii)   Social Security   60
    (iii)   Israeli Sociology   61
    (iv)   Chevra Ve'Revacha   61
References   62

The Evolution of the Israeli Third Sector: A Conceptual and Empirical Analysis

Rachel Calipha
Lecturer, The Academic College of Tel Aviv Yaffo
rachelca@mta.ac.il

Benjamin Gidron
Professor Emeritus, Ben-Gurion University and The College of Management Academic Studies
gidronb@gmail.com

Abstract

The expansion and development of the nonprofit sector worldwide in the 1980s and 1990s did not bypass Israel, and, as in other countries, sparked an interest for study to uncover its characteristics and major features.

The Israeli population—both Jewish and Arab—has a rich tradition of voluntaristic activity on the individual as well as on the collective (organizational) levels, mostly in the communal context. The modern welfare state created new opportunities and new challenges for such activity within the broad framework of the nonprofit sector.

This article aims to review the development of the nonprofit sector in Israel and analyze it within existing nonprofit theories. It takes a historical perspective in looking at its evolution, in light of political, social, ideological, and economic changes in the world and in the country. It discusses the development of policy and government involvement on the one hand and the unique features of Israeli philanthropy, both Jewish and Arab, on the other. It analyzes Israel's civil society and social movements, as well as social entrepreneurship and their expression in the Third Sector. The article also covers the development of research and education on the Third Sector; it includes a review of research centers, databases, journals, and specific programs that were developed by Israeli universities. Finally, this article summarizes the characteristics of the nonprofit sector in Israel.

© RACHEL CALIPHA AND BENJAMIN GIDRON, 2021 | DOI:10.1163/9789004461734_002

Keywords

Israel – civil society – nonprofit sector – third sector – review article – philanthropy – tzedaka – zakat – Arab-Palestinian – policy – academic center – ultra-orthodox – Yishuv – statist – social movements

Editor's Introduction to VR 5.4: Voluntaristics as the Larger Context of the Current *VR* Issue on Nonprofit/Third Sector Research in Israel

Continuing the Editor's long-term plan to have at least one *VR* issue per year reviewing voluntaristics research and theory in a specific country (or related pair of nations, as in the case of *VR* 2.2 on Australia and New Zealand), the present issue *VR* 5.4 reviews voluntaristics research and theory in Israel. The author team of Calipha and Gidron includes the "Father of Israeli Nonprofit Research" (Editor's term), Prof. Ben Gidron. Ben has also been one of the founders of ISTR (International Society for Third Sector Research) and was its first President.

Coined first by the Editor in 2013, *Voluntaristics* is a rather new single-word name (first mentioned publicly in Smith & Sundblom, 2014) for the study of all phenomena relevant to the voluntary, nonprofit, or third sector. The range of phenomena included for study is suggested in Smith (2017, p. 7, paragraph 2). Our global, interdisciplinary, organized field has had many names for over 50 years, as noted in Smith (2017 p. 5), such as Nonprofit Sector and Voluntary Action Research, Nonprofit/Third/Voluntary Sector Research, Philanthropy Studies, Charitable Sector or Tax-Exempt Sector Research, Civil Society Studies or Civil Society Sector Studies, Social Economy or Solidarity Economy Research, Voluntarism/Volunteering/Voluntary Action Research, or Altruistics research, to list the most common names in the research literature.

Voluntaristics has the virtue of being a single word name, like nearly all academic disciplines except political science. The term is also analogous to *linguistics*, as the name for the study of all human languages ever existing. Further, as a neologism, *voluntaristics* is free of any prior connotations or cultural baggage, unlike *philanthropy*, which has strong elitist connotations in English.

A brief overview of what voluntaristics consists of is given in the recent book chapter by Smith (2019). A much longer overview of voluntaristics since its founding in 1971 was given in Smith (2017), which also includes (pp. 52–54) a discussion of the objective reasons why the field has emerged as a *fledgling academic discipline* since about 1995. Many possible reasons for the objective, recent, *exponential* growth of voluntaristics globally since 1995 are listed (pp. 48–51). These 46 possible causal factors are classified into four broad categories: (i) Changes in

Government Regimes and Structures, (ii) Changes in Public Perceptions and Values, (iii) Changes in the Socio-economic Systems within and across Nations, and (iv) Changes in Academia and the Global University System.

There are some important future documents that will expand on what ARNOVA is or should be, and on the larger interdisciplinary field and new academic discipline of voluntaristics:

(1) A special 50th Anniversary issue of *Nonprofit and Voluntary Sector Quarterly* (*NVSQ*), ARNOVA's flagship journal (www.arnova.org) to be published in 2022.

(2) The forthcoming book edited by David. H. Smith and Xinye Wu (forthcoming 2021), *History of Voluntaristics Researcher Associations Globally: How the Global Organized Interdisciplinary Field and Emergent Academic Inter-discipline of Nonprofit/Third/Voluntary Sector, Civil Society, Philanthropy, and Social Economy Studies Was Formed.* [Publisher not yet certain].

(3) The forthcoming book edited by David. H. Smith (and possibly others), (forthcoming 2022), *Voluntaristics and ARNOVA at 50 Years: A Critical Assessment of Their Global Past, Present, and Future.* [Publisher not yet certain].

The current issue of *Voluntaristics Review* touches on nearly all of the structural elements of voluntaristics as an emergent global academic discipline, illustrating for Israel how one important Mediterranean and Middle Eastern nation has encountered these various structural elements or features: interdisciplinary researcher associations, interdisciplinary journals, relevant key books and university graduate theses or dissertations, university-based research centers/ institutes, national and international conferences, college and university courses/majors-concentrations, college and university programs/certificates/ degrees, college and university departments or colleges-schools, faculty position titles reflecting voluntaristics themes in professorships, linkages among universities with voluntaristics activities in the nation and across nations, and persistence of university interest and academic activities in voluntaristics across decades.

References

Smith, David H. (2017). *A Survey of Voluntaristics: Research on the Growth of the Global, Interdisciplinary, Socio-behavioral Science Field and Emergent Inter-discipline.* Leiden, Netherlands, and Boston, MA, USA: Brill.

Smith, David H. (2019). "Voluntaristics: Global Research on NGOs and the Nonprofit Sector." Chapter 14 in *Routledge Handbook of NGOs and International Relations* (193–208), edited by Thomas Davies. London: Routledge.

Smith, David H., & Dan Sundblom. (2014). "Growth of Research-Information Centers, University Departments, and Schools/Colleges in the Emerging Discipline of Voluntaristics-Altruistics." Paper presented at the Annual Conference of ARNOVA, Denver, CO, November 21–23.

Smith, David H., & Xinye Wu (forthcoming 2021). *History of Voluntaristics Researcher Associations Globally: How the Global Organized Interdisciplinary Field and Emergent Academic Inter-discipline of Nonprofit/Third/Voluntary Sector, Civil Society, Philanthropy, and Social Economy Studies Was Formed.* [Publisher not yet certain].

Smith, David H. (and possibly others), (forthcoming 2022). *Voluntaristics and ARNOVA at 50 Years: A Critical Assessment of Their Global Past, Present, and Future.* [Publisher not yet certain].

> *David Horton Smith, Ph.D. (Harvard)*
> Editor-in-Chief, *Voluntaristics Review*
> Research and Emeritus Professor of Sociology, Boston College, Chestnut Hill, MA, USA
> Honorary Visiting Professor of Sociology, School of Arts and Sciences, City, University of London, London, UK
> Honorary Visiting Professor in Sociology, School of Health Sciences, University of East Anglia, Norwich, UK
> Honorary Associated Professor, Centre for Studies of Civil Society and the Nonprofit Sector, National Research University Higher School of Economics, Moscow, Russian Federation
> Visiting Scholar, NGO Research Center and Institute for Philanthropy, Tsinghua University, Beijing, China

[SPECIAL NOTE: This will be the last issue of *VR* as a journal. However, there will continue to be a *Voluntaristics Review Book Series*, under the current Editor.]

1 Introduction[1]

The expansion and development of the nonprofit sector worldwide in the 1980s and 1990s did not bypass Israel, and like in other countries, sparked an interest to study it and uncover its characteristics and major features.

The Israeli population—both Jewish and Arab—has a rich tradition of voluntaristic activity on the individual as well as on the collective (organizational) levels, mostly in the communal context. The modern welfare state created new opportunities and new challenges for such activity within the broad framework of the nonprofit sector.

This article aims to review the development of the nonprofit sector in Israel, analyze it within theoretical formulations, and present data on its major characteristics and features and the development of policy towards it. In the social sciences (as opposed to natural sciences and medicine), practice usually precedes research—we engage in studying and conceptualizing a new social phenomenon after it has been taking place and tried out in the real world. A recent example is the field of startups or impact investment, in which elaborate organizational structures and frameworks in practice have been devised before the academic literature began to deal with it.

The history of the evolution of the Third Sector concept follows a different path,[2] in which research and conceptualization preceded the building structures of practice and policy in this domain. This is true for many countries; but in the Israeli case it is particularly evident. It actually tells the story of how academic research paved the way for the development of policy and practice on the third sector.

The article is divided into ten main sections. The section 2 presents a theoretical analysis of the concept in Israel and ties it to the major theories analyzing the sector. Section 3 discusses the process of the introduction of the *concept* of a Third Sector in Israel. Section 4 presents the major legal and economic dimensions of the sector, while section 5 deals with the concept of civil society and social movements in the Israeli context. Section 6 is devoted to the development of the policy towards the nonprofit sector.

Sections 7 and 8 present an analysis of philanthropy in Israel and that concept in the Arab community. Section 9 discusses social entrepreneurship and social enterprises. Section 10 presents the research and education centers

---

1 We would like to thank Dennis R. Young for his review and his excellent comments to the earlier draft, which helped us improve the article.

2 Obviously nonprofit and voluntary organizations have existed in all cultures for centuries; the focus is on the *concept* of Third Sector—the idea that this diverse group of organizations belong to a unique sector, as is the case with the public and business sectors.

focusing on the Third Sector. Finally, in the Conclusions we summarize the characteristics of the third sector in Israel.

2　Introduction to the Israeli Third Sector: A Theoretical Analysis

The evolution and characteristics of the Israeli Third Sector go hand in hand and can be linked to (1) the country's social and economic history and (2) its population's characteristics.

The following three key factors, related to Israel's social and economic history, can be identified as impacting the nature of the Third Sector and its characteristics.

The first has to do with the fact that Israel was established and developed as the Jewish homeland and follows that ethos. This creates a situation where it is very much linked to its Jewish history, which for 2,000 years took place outside its current borders and is therefore also linked to the current Jewish population in the diaspora. That fact has a major impact on the Third Sector as, for example, most of the philanthropic funds in what we term today Third Sector organizations, found their source historically in the Jewish diaspora (see Section 7 for elaboration).

The second has to do with the fact that most of Israel's initial Jewish immigrants, who settled the land in the early part of the 20th century, came with a strong socialistic ideological background and built institutions along these lines—the Kibbutz being its foremost example. This ideological base had a major impact on the country's ethos in its early years and it was the base of its social-democratic government during the 1950s through the 1980s. During those years, a statist approach and a welfare state policy was followed, which gave the government the ultimate responsibility in steering the economy and society. These conditions limited the evolution of an independent Third Sector, which was, during that period, both dependent on government funding and strict government regulations and policies regarding its functions.

The third has to do with the country's transition, in the mid-1980s, from a corporatist and basically social-democratic economic regime to a neo-liberal one. Given its strong hi-tech industry, developed in the 1990s, Israel was coined as "The Startup Nation" (Senor & Singer, 2009). That ideological and institutional change has started a process of privatization, which caused a growth in the number of Third Sector organizations and their volume of activity, primarily because of a contract regime to provide a multitude of services previously provided by the state. At the same time, with a more liberal economy, a vibrant civil society evolved, with many new and independent Third Sector organizations, in a wide variety of areas and functions that developed. The change of economic regime also impacted significantly the local philanthropy scene. Whereas in the past Israel received philanthropic funds primarily from foreign sources, mostly diaspora Jews, the new economic regime attracted many local successful businesspersons to donate and develop a new culture of philanthropy in the country. It also brought about a change in the management of nonprofit organizations (NPOs), introducing business values, as well as practices and measures of impact relating to their activities.

In addition to those three historical factors, the structure of the Israeli population and its unique characteristics provide added background forces that impact the nature of Israel's Third Sector. These population characteristics actually demonstrate three societal rifts, which are present in everyday life in the country and may erupt from time to time into violent events.

The first rift has to do with Israel's Arab-Palestinian population. While defining itself as a Jewish state, Israel has a sizable Arab minority—some 20 percent of its population. The fact that Israel has not yet settled the dispute with its Palestinian neighbor creates a difficult reality for the Arab citizens as they find themselves in a situation whereby their country is fighting their people. While the Arab-Palestinian population has made tremendous strides into the mainstream of Israeli society, large portions of that population live a traditional way of life and are not integrated into it. This is clearly reflected in the Third Sector; for example in a comparison of the number of civil society organizations per capita between the Jewish and Arab populations and the fact that a lot of the communal activity by Arabs is directed by religious (Muslim and Christian) frameworks.

The second rift has to do with its religious population—especially the ultra-orthodox sector. This population is disconnected from mainstream society, living a traditional way of life in their separate neighborhoods and towns, with their unique educational institutions, not believing in the ethos of a Jewish state, minimizing their contacts with its institutions, and waiting for a Messiah for their salvation. These ultra-orthodox communities, since they do not rely on many of the statutory systems, have developed a dense web of local and communal organizations to care for their different needs as well as a system of philanthropy that can be found in every ultra-orthodox community. This is a well-known pattern from the diaspora, where Jews refused to or were prevented from integrating in the general society and developed their own institutions to care for their needs. The fact that religious parties are part of and often hold the key to a coalition government in Israel, gives that population additional handles to protect their way of life and further their agendas.

Finally, the third rift has to do with its ethnic heterogeneity. Israel gathered immigrants from more than seventy countries and has been for many years a rich tapestry of cultures and viewpoints. Obviously with time and intermarriages a lot of that has been lost, but a split still exists between children and grandchildren of immigrants from the Middle East (North Africa, Iraq, Syria), called Mizrachi (or Sephardi) and those from Europe and North America (Ashkenazi). The fact that Israel's cultural, political, and economic foundations were mostly created by the latter, left the descendants of the former with feelings of discrimination. That rift has a major expression in the cultural life and the media, but less so in the Third Sector, where an analysis along these lines will not yield significant results.

Given all these features, the challenge is to analyze the Israeli Third Sector within existing Third Sector theories or to challenge those. We will do so using both the Social Origins theory (Salamon & Anheier, 1998), which analyzes the features of the sector in light of societal forces that shape it. We will also be using the Third Sector Roles Theory (Young & Casey, 2017) to analyze the evolution of the sector's role. Both of these can be done after introducing a periodic analysis of Israeli society in the past 140 years.[3]

In the literature on the history of the Israeli Third Sector it is common to divide it into three distinctive periods (Gidron, 1997; Limor, 2004; Silber & Rosenhek, 2000):

The first period, the pre-state (Yishuv): 1880–1948. In the absence of sovereignty, the leaders of the Jewish community built and expanded an elaborate organizational network that both represented the different political and ideological factions of the Yishuv and dealt with its members' social, educational, and health needs. Funding for these organizations came primarily from the Jewish diaspora.

The second period, the formative era: 1948–mid-1970s. This was characterized by a transfer of the responsibility to provide social, educational, and health services from the ideologically based (Third Sector) organizations to the state. As the population rejoiced in the fact that a Jewish state was finally established, a statist ideology replaced the multitude of ideologies that had governed Israeli society before. There was hardly any political dissent and protest. Third Sector organizations basically functioned as an arm of government, providing semi-public services and did not engage in challenging government policies.

The third period, from the late 1970s onward. This can be termed the "Pluralist era," during which the collectivistic ideologies were replaced by values that stressed individualism, liberalism, and particularism, which coincided with the loss of power of the Labor Party to the right-wing Likud Party. New types of organizations were developed: Small and medium-size, focusing on

---

3 Israel gained independence in 1948, but it is common to analyze the start of Israeli society's history at the beginning of the first Zionist immigration, in 1882.

particular issues, representing new constituencies and needs, and depending for their existence less on public funding than in the previous era. In addition, during this period the "Law of Amutot (Associations) 1980" was approved (see Section 4), and since then we have witnessed an increase in the number of registrations of new NPOs. The Third Sector during this period became more heterogeneous, representing different populations and new issues—some in opposition to government policies. In general, as in other countries, the sector can be described as consisting of (1) mostly public or semi-public service providing organizations, connected to the state and funded by it, to a large extent through contractual arrangements; and (2) independent organizations of the civil society, dealing with a variety of issues, not guided by the state and do not necessarily receive funding from it (Almog-Bar & Greenspan, 2019).

Gidron, Bar, and Katz, in their book *The Israeli Third Sector* (2004), devote a section in their "Summary and Conclusions" chapter to theoretical analysis. They find the demand-side economic theories less relevant to the Israeli case, but the supply-side theory (James, 1987) can explain certain features. James suggests that Third Sector organizations are established in order to attract potential adherents to a particular religious or political ideology. This clearly explains the establishment of many service-providing organizations during the pre-state period. "During that time, the various ideological movements established service-providing third sector organizations in order to obtain political support. Later, in the 1980s and 1990s the Shas (religious) party and the Islamic movement employed similar tactics" (p. 168).

The authors find the social origins theory, which focuses on a variety of influences (not just economic) on the structure of the sector more applicable to the Israeli case. The theory, which analyzes specific forces in the country's history and their interactions, suggests that certain combinations in those interactions shape the nature of the Third Sector in Israel. The authors do however modify the specific forces identified by Salamon and Anheier (1998). Whereas the social origins theory identifies the Church, the state, the trade unions, and the urban bourgeoisie as the forces shaping the features of the Third Sector in many (primarily European) countries, in Israel an urban bourgeoisie cannot be counted as a factor. In addition to religion, state, and trade unions, a fourth factor identified was diaspora philanthropy. Those four forces, each of which had a different impact on the nature of the Sector during the different periods (Salamon & Anheier, 1998, pp. 169–170).

A later article (Kabalo, 2009) elaborates on this conceptualization and further modifies the social origins theory as it pertains to Israel (and additional non-European countries). Whereas Salamon and Anheier use their formulation and follow Esping-Andersen (1990) to develop four types of Third Sector regimes, Israel fitting into a corporatist one, Kabalo departs from such a

European-centered formulation and relates the structure and functions of the Third Sector to the concept of nation-building, mostly of countries which received their independence after 1945. Kabalo highlights the associative life in the country before and after independence, given that the colonizing forces were not interested in providing social services to the local populations. The Third Sector in such countries was a part of the struggle for independence during the colonial era and a part of nation-building, collaborating with the newly established independent government.

It is important to stress that social origins theory has been recently criticized (Anheier, Lang, & Toepler, 2020). They propose "a comparative-historical research agenda informed by political science and sociology to complement the macroeconomic approach, based on national income accounting, that has dominated the field for nearly three decades" (p. 675) and they suggest to connect the field of comparative nonprofit sector research to the wider social science research agenda, especially those related to Varieties of Democracy (V-Dem) and Varieties of Capitalism approaches, which makes sense in the Israeli case, with all its complexities.

The theoretical literature on the Third Sector was enriched in the 1990s by the introduction of the civil society concept, so as to stress the associative, entrepreneurial and participatory functions of nonprofit organizations, in addition to their service-provision functions. This directs the researcher toward the disciplines of sociology and political science rather than economics and law, when studying the phenomenon of the Third Sector. Thus, Gidron, Bar, and Katz (2004) have used that approach to analyze the Third Sector data on Israel. They analyze the evolution of the Israeli Third Sector according to Foley and Edwards' (1996) categorization of civil society I and II. Whereas civil society I is an independent domain separate from the state, pluralistic, involves voluntary action, and participatory citizen activity, civil society II is perceived as a domain which includes entities with the goal of changing the political and social order. Civil society I, with a high degree of independence, barely existed in Israel during the pre-state and the statist eras, and only developed in the 1980s, when individualism sank in as a "legitimate" value, instead of the previous collectivistic approach. At that time many new organized initiatives were introduced in the form of civil society organizations as well as new independent funding sources—including international ones, not controlled by the central government.

Civil society II types of organizations were clearly present during the pre-state era, when they supported the different underground organizations that fought for independence and attempted to end the colonial regime. During the Statist era little anti-government activity was recorded by the civil society.

THE EVOLUTION OF THE ISRAELI THIRD SECTOR

An increase in activity to change the political order has been observed since the 1980s, especially as a result or in the aftermath of crises. Those usually have taken place after demonstrations by frustrated citizens. Such events took place after Arab demonstrations in October 2000, after the economic crisis of 2008, and in 2020 by groups of citizens demonstrating against the government both because of allegations of corruption by the Prime Minister and because of the economic hardships caused by COVID-19. These spontaneous demonstrations are often organized by civil society organizations critical of the government or of specific government policies.

Another theoretical formulation relevant to analyze the Israeli Third Sector is Young and Casey's (2017) analysis of the roles of the sector, especially in its relationships with government. Young and Casey present three types of possible relationships between the Third Sector and government: (1) Supplementary, when nonprofits are seen as fulfilling demand for public goods left unsatisfied by government; (2) complementary, when nonprofits are seen as partners to government, helping to deliver public goods largely financed by government, and (3) adversarial, when nonprofits prod government to make changes in public policy and to maintain accountability to the public (p. 33). Young and Casey add that these roles and formats of relationships are not mutually exclusive and can exist simultaneously between government and the Sector.

Actually, a slightly different perspective on roles was applied to the Israeli case by Ralph Kramer already in the 1980s (Kramer, 1981). In his comparative studies of voluntary organizations in the welfare field, Kramer identified four potential roles that these organizations fill: Vanguard/innovator, advocacy, value guardian, service provider. In Kramer's study in Israel (1976), which formed part of his 1981 comparative study (which was performed during the Statist era, with public services that cherished the professional ethos and were less concerned with upholding the value of voluntarism or advocacy), he found little of that in the voluntary organizations he studied. They filled primarily the role of supplementary service provision for populations for whom public services did not exist.

Using Young's formulation during the three different periods in the evolution of the sector, it is clear that during the pre-state era, in the absence of a service-providing public sector, voluntary (nonprofit) organizations provided social, educational, and health services to the population, acting basically in a supplementary role. During the Statist era, when government agencies took over the service provision responsibilities, nonprofits acted primarily in a complementary role, providing services coordinated with the public service provision mechanisms, and the adversarial role was rarely performed. During the pluralistic era that picture changes. The breaking of the collectivistic approach brought about a focus on individualism and an emphasis on particular needs and tastes—in education, culture, health, and so on. This was translated into a variegated Third Sector that was involved in filling all three roles: It supplemented government services and established new services where these did not exist (e.g., specialized museums, shelters for battered women); it complemented government services and coordinated their provision within a system of contracts, and finally it acted in an adversarial role in opposing policies of discrimination (against women, the LGBT community, refugees, etc.) or those of political controversy (e.g., settlements in the West Bank). Furthermore, the question of curbing certain adversarial features of the sector are discussed by the government from time to time, which is a sign of the vitality of this role. Thus, the Israeli Third Sector is clearly a diversified one; its nature evolved and developed over the years and the theoretical formulations help express it.

3 The Introduction of the Third Sector *Concept* in Israel

3.1 *The Early Beginnings: The 1970s and 1980s*

The history of the research activity in Israel on what is known today as the Third Sector started by studying that category of organizations before it was conceptualized as a sector. The person who deserves the right of first to engage in such work is undoubtedly Ralph Kramer. Kramer, a professor at the School of Social Welfare at the University of California in Berkeley, studied voluntary organizations as a distinct category in Israel during the 1970s and 1980s.

In his first study (Kramer, 1970), he analyzed and compared the practice of community work in the Netherlands and Israel. Following this research, he became interested in the influence that Israeli voluntary organizations have on social policy. He identified four organizational roles such organizations fill: (1) *Vanguard*—innovate, pioneer, experiment, and demonstrate programs, some of which eventually will be taken by the government, (2) *Improver or advocate*, the roles of critic or watchdog as it pressures a governmental body to extend, improve, or establish needed services, (3) *Value guardian*, of voluntaristic, particularistic, and sectarian values, promoting citizen participation, develop leadership, protecting the special interests of social, religious, cultural, or other minority groups, (4) *Service provider*, delivering certain services it has selected, some of which may be a public responsibility that government is unable, unwilling, or prefers not to assume directly or fully (Kramer, 1981, p. 9).

In another study, he examined fifteen Israeli voluntary agencies serving the physically and mentally disabled (Kramer, 1976). He identified problems in their filling the roles of citizen participation, innovation, and promotion of social change. In a follow-up study (Kramer, 1984), he examined the voluntary agencies in a perspective of ten years (1972–82). He found a pattern of a stable growth and concluded that the agencies managed to thrive and not only to survive, despite the unstable environment.

These studies laid the foundations for the development of the future research on the Third Sector along several aspects:

1. The basic conception regarding the role of voluntary organizations, according to which their activities have an importance that goes beyond being frameworks for the provision of services.
2. The relationship between the voluntary organizations and the government beyond the funding issue.
3. The studies he conducted in Israel were part of comparative studies in other countries and paved the way for the great comparative studies of the 1990s.
4. His research orientation, social welfare, stood out in his articles and books and this has influenced, among others, the researchers in this field in Israel.

Following Kramer, Katan (1988) and Eran (1992) examined the roles of voluntary organizations, whether substitute or partner in the welfare state. Still in the 1980s and following Kramer, three researchers discovered the field of voluntary organizations as an area of their specialization and published papers on that topic:

Eliezer Jaffe, a professor at the School of Social Work at the Hebrew University, has been engaged in an attempt to create a categorization of organizations, especially in the field of welfare (Jaffe, 1982, 1983). He focuses on an important subcategorization of philanthropic funds (Jaffe, 1979) and to the traditional (mostly Jewish) foreign funding patterns of third sector organizations in Israel (Jaffe, 1985, 1987).

Yael Yishai, a professor of Political Science at Haifa University, studied voluntary organizations from a political science disciplinary perspective. In her early work, she also analyzed a specific category of organizations—interest groups—and points out their social and political roles (Yishai, 1987).

Benjamin Gidron, a professor of Social Work at Ben-Gurion University, conducted a joint study with David Bargal on self-help groups, as well as a comparative study on this topic with Mark Chesler (Gidron, 1984; Gidron & Bargal, 1986; Gidron & Chesler, 1994).

In all those studies of the 1980s and early 1990s, the leading concept was "voluntary associations/organizations," which was the basis on which research was built.

3.2 The Conferences that Changed the Picture

The studies mentioned above, as well as the development of new ideologies regarding the privatization of public services and the renewed debate on the welfare state, led to the first international conference in Israel on this topic. This conference, "Volunteers, Voluntary Action, Public Policy," was held in Kibbutz Kiryat Anavim, on May 22–24, 1989. It was organized by Benjamin Gidron, Ralph Kramer (who was staying in Israel on his sabbatical), and Israel Katz, the former Minister of Labor and Social Welfare.

The conference revealed to the Israeli researchers the new thinking and the new paradigms in the field. It also showcased research in Israel to colleagues around the world, an exposure whose results were seen in the decade of the 1990s, when various Israeli researchers were integrated into international research projects.

This conference and the earlier one in Bad Honnef, Germany (1986), as well as the subsequent conference in Indianapolis, USA (1992)—where the International Society for Third-Sector Research (ISTR) was founded—were the backdrop to the development of the Johns Hopkins International Classification of Nonprofit Organizations (ICNPO) mapping project.

3.3 The Johns Hopkins Project

The *International Classification of Nonprofit Organizations*, conducted by Lester Salamon and Helmut Anheier (Salamon et al., 1999) at the Institute for Civil Society Research (currently the Center for Civil Society) at Johns Hopkins University, is rightfully considered a crucial breakthrough in the systematic knowledge development of the Third Sector worldwide. The project sought to examine, and if possible, measure, six dimensions of the Third Sector in each of the participating countries. These were: Its definition, economic data, legal structure, history, public policy in relation to the sector, and patterns of public contribution and volunteering. The basis of the study was a common definition of a Third Sector organization—the structural-operational definition (Salamon et al, 1999, pp. 3–4), which made it possible not only to collect data on the activity of the sector in the various countries but also to conduct international comparative research.

Israel joined the Johns Hopkins Project in 1996, in its second stage. The invitation to join came during the first stage, but at that time no funding was obtained for participation. However, preparations for the study began in 1992–93, when Benjamin Gidron, in collaboration with the National Accounting Division of the Central Bureau of Statistics, conducted a survey of the income and expenses of nonprofit organizations in the nonprofit department and public income tax institutions, in accordance with the criteria and metrics developed by the Johns Hopkins Project. This was the first time such data were collected and systematically analyzed.

This was a great opportunity to get to know the state of the data in the field and the difficulty in obtaining them. When the budget for the inclusion of Israel in the international project (from the Yad Hanadiv and the Kahanoff Foundations) was obtained, a certain infrastructure of data and working methods already existed.

As part of the project, expert research teams were established for each of the six dimensions, and they studied and published their findings. The publications (Bar-Mor, 1999; Gidron, 1997; Gidron & Katz, 1998; Gidron, Katz, & Bar, 2003, 1999; Gidron et al., 2003; Shay et al., 1999; Silber & Rosenhek, 2000; Telias, Katan, & Gidron, 2000) were published in the framework of the Israeli Center for Third Sector Research (ICTR) at Ben-Gurion University (see Section 10 and Appendix V), which was established in 1997 and served as a formal host for the Johns Hopkins Project.

The Johns Hopkins Project not only presented to the Israeli research community, policy-makers, and the general public the *concept* of the Third Sector as a new organizing principle and a new lens through which to view reality, but also provided basic data on its dimensions in a comparative perspective. This gave an impetus to develop both research and policy along this new concept as is shown in this article. Furthermore, by its classification into different fields of practice—education, health, welfare, environment, and so on—it provided a detailed picture of its nature.

4 Legal and Economic Characteristics of the Israeli Third Sector

Based on the findings from the Johns Hopkins Project and ensuing studies, it is possible to paint a picture of the major characteristics of the Israeli Third Sector.

4.1 *The Legal Dimension*
The laws of incorporation in Israel allow organizations to register as a nonprofit corporation through a number of venues: The Law of Associations, 1980; The Public Companies' Law, 1999; the Cooperative Societies Ordinance;

The major one is the Law of Amutot (Associations) (Limor, 2004, 2008).

The Law of Amutot states (in section 19) that each association must have at least three institutions:

(1)   General Meeting;

(2)   Board of Directors;

(3)   An Audit Committee (or an auditing body that may be an accountant or other body approved by a Registrar Associations).

In nonprofit organizations with a turnover of more than NIS 1 million (the exact amount is updated annually), there is an obligation, in addition to the above, to appoint an accountant, for the purpose of auditing the association's financial report. In nonprofit organizations with a turnover of more than NIS 10 million, there is an obligation, in addition to the above, to appoint an internal auditor.

The association should set its rules and goals at the time of its establishment. Any change requires the approval of the Registrar. The Registrar of Associations has the duty to examine: (1) If the association meets all the requirements of the law, and (2) if the association's assets and income are used for the purposes of the association only. If they do the association gets the certificate known as "Proper Management Approval". In 1998 the Israeli government decided that bodies applying for support from a government ministry would be required to present the "Proper Management Approval" from the Registrar of Associations.

The Duty of Disclosure Act was enacted in 2011, regarding organizations supported by a foreign political entity. The associations have to report on foreign donations.

As part of the Registrar of Associations' annual work plan, the Registrar conducts in-depth audits in the associations, through accounting firms that act as external auditors on his behalf. The purpose of the audit is to examine the association's activities and compliance with the provisions of the law, the provisions of its rules, and its objectives.

The authority of the Registrar of Associations is to impose administrative fines for breach of duties, both on associations and on committee members who are responsible for breach of duties. These amendments to the Law of Associations actually increase, through administrative measures, the level of control of the Registrar over the Third Sector organizations.

Additional laws refer to: (1) The Real Estate Taxation Law, which includes special provisions for nonprofits; (2) The Property Tax Act, which allows for a full exemption for a public institution that meets the conditions set by law; (3) "Municipal Taxation"—exemptions from property taxes that originate in the Mandatory Ordinance; (4) Fees—associations are required to pay an annual fee (Limor, 2008).

In addition, there are laws providing benefits to donors. The benefit given to a donor in Israel allows a tax credit in respect of a contribution to an organization with a certificate in accordance with section 46; that is, the tax-payer is entitled to the amount of the contribution within the limits of the calculation formula, from the total tax owed. The calculation formula determines a floor and a ceiling for a contribution that qualifies for a tax credit, within the limits according to which the credit will be at the rate of 35 percent of the total contribution and will not exceed 30 percent of the total taxable income or NIS 4 million, whichever is lower (Limor, 2008).

4.2 *The Economic Dimension*

The first institution to measure the economic data of nonprofit organizations (NPOS) was the National Statistical Bureau (NSB) that analyzed 1982 data, which did not include data on organizations that registered according to the Law of Associations (1980). Later, Gidron (1999) examines the economic data by using a sample of 1,331 NPO which filed income tax returns for 1991, and compared between the studies' findings. In 1999, a Third Sector database was inaugurated at Ben-Gurion University of the Negev, which integrated data from various governmental sources (the Associations Registrar, Income Tax, the General Comptroller of the Ministry of Finance, among others). This database has been used by later studies (Gidron, 1999; Gidron & Alon, 2004; Gidron & Katz, 1999; Katz, Gidron & Limor, 2009). Other studies combined NSB data and Income Tax, such as Katz & Yogev-Keren (2013), who examined the Third Sector workforce. In 2010, comprehensive database of the Third Sector was published for the public in GuideStar website (see Section 10 and Appendix V). Based on this data, Almog-Bar and Greenspan (2019) presented the status of the Third Sector in 2016.

The initial economic picture based on the Johns Hopkins Project's findings did not change drastically throughout the years. The Israeli Third Sector was found to be very large in economic terms—roughly 5–8 percent of Israel's GDP is channeled through Third Sector organizations and a similar figure pertains to the workforce. This has to do with the sector's traditional proximity to the government and its important service-delivery functions, similarly to other corporatist arrangements in many European countries.

4.2.1 Current Economic Data

According to the NSB database, nonprofit represented 4.5 percent of Israel's GDP in 2017–18 (early estimates), and 5.3 percent in 2016.

According to the Israeli NPOS' Yearbook (2020), the total income of all NPOS in 2018 was NIS 93.4 billon. It includes 34 percent (NIS 31.7 billion) from supports and endowments from the state, 7 percent (NIS 6.1 billion) from services sale to government parties, 37 percent (NIS 34.9 billion) from services' sale to non-government parties, 13 percent (NIS 12.3 billion) from donations from

Israel, and 9 percent (NIS 8.4 billion) from donations from abroad (for more details, see Appendix 1).

In summary, the total income includes 41 percent revenues from the government and 59 percent revenues from private parties.

The NPOs operate in a wide geographic distribution: 26 percent (4,319) have a nationwide deployment; 22 percent (3,652) in Jerusalem; 9 percent (1,447) in the North; 7 percent (1,078) in Haifa; 20 percent (3,262) in the Center; 13 percent (2,198) in Tel Aviv; 10 percent (1,617) in the South; and 7 percent (1,164) in Judea and Samaria. (Note: The percentages do not add up to 100 percent as there are associations that operate in more than one district.)

The NPOs' areas of activity are divided into eleven categories. Of the 16,469 active associations (15,847 associations and 622 Community Interest Company ("Chevra Letoelet Hazibur")) in 2018, the distribution was as follows: 36 percent (5,942) religion; 24 percent (3,935) culture, sport, and leisure; 18 percent (2,989) research and education; 11 percent (1,794) welfare services; 4 percent (592) health; 2 percent (279) volunteering and philanthropy; 2 percent (268) professional associations; 2 percent (251) advocacy; 1 percent (230) development and housing; 0.9 percent (151) environment; and 0.2 percent (38) international activity. (Note: percentages rounded up.)

Of the total revenue of NIS 93.4 billion, 38 percent (35,107 million) was concentrated in education and research associations, 15 percent (14,151 million) in culture, sports, and leisure, 14 percent (12,784 million) in health, 11 percent (9,891 million) in welfare services, 8 percent (7,724 million) in religion, 8 percent (7,519 million) in philanthropy and volunteering, 4 percent (3,788 million) housing and development, 1 percent (1,239 million) in advocacy, 0.8 percent (761 million) in trade unions, 0.4 percent (376 million) in the environment, and 0.03 percent (31 million) in international activities. (Note: percentages rounded up.)

4.2.2   Employees and Volunteers

According to the Israeli NPOs' Yearbook (2020), there were 633,673 men and women employees in Third Sector organizations in 2018: 49 percent (311,538) employed in research and education associations, 21 percent (133,220) in culture, sports and leisure associations, 12 percent (73,785) in welfare associations, 9 percent (55,517) in health, 6 percent (38,938) in religion, 1 percent (7,916) in housing and development, 0.7 percent (4,511) in philanthropy and volunteering, 0.5 percent (3,388) in advocacy, 0.5 percent (2,929) in professional unions, 0.3 percent (1,859) in environment, and international activity employed only 0.01 percent (72) employees. (Note: percentages rounded up.)

During the same year there were 710,331 men and women volunteers: 28 percent (197,634) active in welfare associations, 27 percent (192,010) in research and development associations, 17 percent (120,656) in culture, sports, and leisure associations, 14 percent (96,144) in health, 6 percent (38,887) in religion, 5 percent (36,507) in philanthropy and volunteering, 1 percent (9,089) in advocacy, 1 percent (8,979) in environment, 0.9 percent (6,261) in housing and development, 0.5 percent (3,741) in professional associations, and in international activity only 0.1 percent (423). (Note: percentages rounded up.)

As to the classification of the associations by size—altogether there are 8,250 (23 percent) small, 6,600 (27 percent) medium and 1,650 (39 percent) large associations. Small associations are defined as those with revenues that range from NIS 0–400,000 per year; medium-sized associations are those with revenues ranging from NIS 400,000–7.6 million and large associations are those with revenues from NIS 7.6 million–2.6 billion. Small associations have an average of one employee and twelve volunteers; medium associations have an average of seventeen employees and twenty-eight volunteers and large associations an average of 313 employees and 259 volunteers.

Moreover, the ratio of workers to volunteers is very different between the groups: in small associations, more volunteers are employed than in salaried medium-sized organizations since for every two employees on average there are three volunteers; whereas in large nonprofits the ratio is reversed, so that on average every four volunteers has five employees. These data suggest that small associations rely heavily on volunteering, while large associations rely more on paid work.

4.2.3 Characteristics of Workforce

The latest comprehensive research on workforce was done by Katz and Yogev-Keren (2013). The finding shows that the labor force in the Third Sector is relatively young and educated, and that there is over-representation of women (68 percent). In addition, despite a slow decentralization process, most of the employment is concentrated in the center (Tel Aviv and Jerusalem districts) and not in the periphery.

Despite a moderate but stable upward trend in the number of employees in the sector, it is clear that the employment market in the Third Sector is not one that guarantees job security: rapid turnover of employees is a feature of the sector—61 percent of employees are employed for less than two years in the organization. In addition, there is a considerable multiplicity of temporary and part-time jobs, as well as regular and stable seasonal patterns—a decrease of 20 percent in the volume of work is notable during the summer months and the High Holidays season.

An examination of the share of wages paid from work in nonprofit organizations in relation to the total individual income from work in that year shows that the average wage ratio was 62 percent. This figure means that on average, an individual's income from a job in the Third Sector constitutes only 62 percent of his total income from work in that year. That is, the existing employment structure in the sector forces its workers to supplement income from work in other places.

The average monthly wage per job paid by Third Sector organizations is significantly lower than the average wage per employee job in the general economy. The figures in 2009 were NIS 4,230 in the Third Sector as opposed to NIS 8,131 in the general economy. That same year, the average salary of managers in the Third Sector was NIS 17,047. The authors of the report suggest that those figures follow an international trend whereby salaries in the Third Sector are significantly lower than the general average, mostly because of the practice to hire employees in part-time positions.

5   Civil Society and Social Movements—The Associational Perspective

The "Hopkins Project" emphasized the economic aspects of third sector activity, especially its service delivery functions but neglects the meaning of voluntary incorporation patterns in society. The research paradigm that focuses on these aspects, such as voluntary incorporation patterns, known as 'Civil Society,' was developed parallel to the Hopkins Project. Anheier defined 'Civil Society': "An independent space that includes institutions, organizations, social networks, and individuals (and the values they bring with them), located between the areas of activity of the family, the state and the market, and characterized by a set of civic rules where people voluntarily unite to advance common goals and interests" (2004, 22). Another study distinguished among countries between 'Civil Society I' and 'Civil Society II' (Foley & Edwards, 1996). This latter distinction applied also within a country (Minkoff, 1997); it distinguishes between organizations that oppose the government and organizations that don't necessarily criticize the government but deal with issues different than government. Concepts such as "political and social change" (Ben Eliezer, 1999; Fogiel-Bijaoui, 1998; Gidron, 2007) and "democracy of social capital" (Gidron, 2007; Yishai, 2003) are also discussed in the context of third sector.

5.1   *The Associational Perspective: Organizations of the Civil Society in Israel*

Over the years, lots of associations and Community Interest Company ("Chevra Letoelet Hazibur") have been registered, however some have been disbanded or deleted, while some are still registered but are not active, and others are active but do not have valid management certificate.

According to the Israeli NPOS' Yearbook (2020), 61,412 associations have been registered since the beginning of the documentation on Guidestar in 2010, 23,694 have been disbanded or deleted, and 37,448 associations are now registered. Of all the registered associations, 19,205 are active associations in 2020 (associations that have submitted legal reports to the Registrar of Associations in the last three years), of which 13,161 are associations with a valid management certificate (approval given only to associations that have applied and met the required conditions, and can only be granted after two years of activity). 1,580 Community Interest Companies have ever been registered, of which 1,425 are registered in 2020. Of all the registered, 743 are active and 513 have a valid management certificate.

Between 2015 and 2019, an average of 1,763 associations and sixty-nine Community Interest Companies were registered each year. The highest registration was in the field of religion (441 associations), followed by culture, sports, and leisure (423 associations), and in the field of welfare services (378 associations). In the other areas, fewer than 69 associations were registered on average each year.

5.2 Sources of Funding

There are three sources of funding in Israeli NPOS: the government, sale to private parties, and donations. Revenues from the state include funds transferred from the government, local authorities, and other government units in two ways: Support funds and allowances; funds paid to nonprofits for the provision of services to the public, as part of contracts with them. According to the Israeli NPOS' Yearbook (2020), in half of the associations (except for the field of education and research), the revenues from public sources accounted for 21 percent or more of the association's total income. In other areas, at least half of the associations had no revenues from the state in 2018.

Some of the state's revenues are revenues from the Support Budget under Article 3A of the Budget Basics Law, 1985. Another channel through which associations receive funds from the state is via grants from the Social Security funds. The grants are given by the five Social Security funds—the Disability Fund, the Nursing Fund, the Children's Fund, the Special Enterprises Fund, and the Manof Fund (for more details, see Appendix 11).

Revenues from the sale of services to private entities includes consideration for the provision of services to individuals and households, other nonprofit organizations, businesses, and in fact to any non-governmental entity. They also include membership fee income and other income such as interest. According to the NPOS' Yearbook (2020), half of the professional unions (associations of a group that is engaged in a particular field in order to represent and promote their interest) relied solely on sales to private entities, meanwhile in half of the housing and development associations, 40 percent or more of the income was received from sales to private parties, and half of the nonprofit organizations in religion, philanthropy, and volunteering and welfare services had no revenue from sales to private individuals.

Donations include those by Israelis and from abroad, including grants from foundations. Donations were the most common source of funding in 2018, in the sense that except for the field of professional unions, half of the associations in each field received some donations, and in most areas, donations were the main source of funding for at least half of the associations. For example, in half of the associations in each of the fields of religion, philanthropy, and volunteering and welfare services 99 percent or more of the income was received from donations. In half of the advocacy associations, 85 percent or more of the income was received from donations, and in half of the internationally active nonprofit organizations, 81 percent or more of the income was received from donations.

One of the most important tools in policy to encourage donations as an instrument to strengthen organizations that operate in a competitive environment is tax credit in return for donations (see Section 7 and Appendix III). In addition, associations must report grants and donations from a foreign political entity (for details, see Appendix II).

5.3   *Social Movements*

Social movements are defined as networks of informal interactions between a plurality of individuals, groups, and/or organizations, engaged in political or cultural conflicts, on the basis of shared collective identities (Diani, 1992). In Israel there are several groups that feel discriminated against and have created organizations to oppose this. The most prominent ones are: (1) Women, (2) Arabs, who constitute 21 percent of the population (Israel's Independence Day, 2019), (3) the Ultra-Orthodox (Haredi) community that has chosen to erect "walls of sanctity" and separate itself in certain aspects from mainstream Israeli society (Malach & Cahaner, 2018, p. 1), (4) the lesbian, gay, bisexual, and transgender (LGBT) community (Tel Aviv is known as a "Gay Capital of the Middle East"—Gay Israel, 2019), (5) the Ethiopian community. These groups suffer mainly from inequality and racism. Each of them is fighting for its rights in different ways, including protests.

The Association for Civil Rights in Israel carried out a representative survey in 2014 of the Israeli public and found that when asked which groups are likely to be targets of racism, Ethiopians were mentioned by 79 percent, Arabs by 68 percent, and the Ultra-Orthodox community by almost 42 percent of the respondents (The Association for Civil Rights in Israel, 2014). Israel ranks low in terms of tolerance of LGBTQ people and support for equal rights for the community, according to the European Social Survey (Lior, 2015).

The Berl Katzenelson Foundation and the Vigo company developed the Hate Index. This index is based on a monitoring system that scans posts from social media channels (e.g., Facebook, Twitter, blogs, forums, and comment sections) on a daily basis. They looked for phrases that contain racist, violent, or offensive content, and calls for violence. They found that the groups that were targeted most (with the most offensive phrases) were Arabs and the Ultra-Orthodox community (Berl Katzenelson Foundation Report, 2019, published in *Haaretz*, 2019).

Each of these populations has created its own social movements, organizations, and advocacy organizations (see Appendix II). The funding of such organizations is of course key to their survival, as by and large they would not qualify to receive funding from public sources, because of their oppositional stance to government policies and the fact that they raise issues the government is not interested in. It is not surprising, therefore, that in many instances such organizations have to turn to funding sources abroad (see Gidron, Katz, & Hasenfeld, 2002).

A major funding source for such organizations (those that promote social justice for all) for the past four decades has been the New Israel Fund (NIF)—a foundation which started as a coalition of liberal Israelis and American Jews, but has expanded since and has supporters from many countries. Its founders envisioned an Israel that reflected their progressive values. The NIF states it is working to build a stronger democracy in Israel, rooted in the values of equality, of inclusion, and of social justice. Through the years it has supported a variety of organizations of the different categories listed above. Furthermore, it has a consulting arm, Shatil, which helps social movement organizations to solve management problems and it also creates coalitions among similar entities.

6 Policy Development towards the Third Sector

The development of policy towards the Third Sector in Israel can be divided into three periods. The first refers to the 1990s. This period is characterized by a lack of recognition of the civil society and the Third Sector (Gidron, 1997; Gidron, Bar, & Katz, 2004; Gidron & Katz, 2001; Yishai, 1998), as well as by a privatization of the public services (Katan, 2007). The second period refers to the years 2000–08 (Almog-Bar, 2016). It includes the following important events: The Galnoor Committee (Galnoor, et al., 2003), The Round Tables

Project, The Aridor Committee (Israel Prime Minister's Office 2006), The Lebanon War (Katz et al., 2007), and The Government Report (Israel Prime Ministers' Office, 2008). The third period takes in the implications of the 2008 Economic Crisis (Almog-Bar, 2016; Weinheber, 2011; Weinheber, Sembira, & Oz-Ari, 2015).

6.1   Lack of Recognition

Gidron and Katz were surprised to find the initial lack of documentation on government funding of the Sector, which meant that funding was not systematic and lacked a clear policy. They start their introduction as follows (Gidron, & Katz, 2001):

> When one reviews the issue of government policy vis-à-vis the third sector in Israel, one immediately encounters a major paradox. While nonprofit organizations handle important areas of public life and receive very significant amounts of public funding, there is no clear or stated policy towards these organizations as a distinct category, nor has the government established to date a public body to develop such policy. The sector's current status has evolved over the years from responses to historical processes, constraints, and pressures of various kinds rather than from a comprehensive and well-developed concept of the sector's role. Laws, ordinances, regulations, and procedures governing the activities of nonprofit organizations exist and define the relationships between these organizations and governmental authorities; however, it is practically impossible to identify any documents that provide the basis for these laws and regulations. Yet, the fact that very significant governmental funds are allocated to nonprofit organizations—a trend that has developed over many years—indicates a de facto policy that is dynamic—it develops and changes. Such changes generally have resulted from a specific governmental authority's action or a Supreme Court intervention in response to a concrete situation requiring attention, usually in a certain area of practice (i.e., higher education, health) or a particular set of organizations (i.e., Yeshivot—Torah institutes). In all those cases, these changes were not based on comprehensive discussion in the government or the Knesset regarding policy toward the sector as a whole, and pertained only to the specific situation under consideration. The lack of any formal documents regarding government policy vis-à-vis the third sector makes it impossible to find an official rationale for developing a formal relationship with these organizations.
>
> (GIDRON & KATZ, 2001, p. 1135)

6.2   *The Galnoor Committee*

In light of the lack of policy towards the Third Sector and given the data collected on the Third Sector in Israel within the Johns Hopkins Project, the Israeli Center for Third Sector Research (ICTR) initiated the establishment of a public committee of experts and stakeholders to look into the matter and devise a report regarding a desired policy towards this category of organization. Prof. Itzhak Galnoor of Hebrew University accepted the invitation to chair the committee, which comprised Advocate Ariella Ophir, Prof. Arieh Arnon, Michal Bar, Yoram Gabai, Prof. Benjamin Gidron, Bassel Ghatas, Sarah Silberstein, Adv. Ophir Katz, Rachel Liel, Nissan Limor, Walid Moulla, Amir Mahoul, Adv. Avi Armoni, Prof. Yosef Katan, Varda Shiffer, and Dr. Emanuel Sharon.

The following description summarized the committee stages published by The Israeli Center for Third Sector Research (Brochure, 2004):

> The committee's work proceeded in two phases. In the first, the focus was on specific topics related to policy toward the third sector and "expert witnesses" were invited to attend specific sessions. In the second phase, the committee's work focused on the prevailing situation, on drawing conclusions and on shaping their findings. The committee's work was accompanied by research into policies adopted towards the third sector in four countries worldwide, which added an international perspective to its work in Israel.

The committee found that the number of Third Sector organizations operating in Israel since the 1980s has markedly increased and that their operations have considerably multiplied. These dramatic changes have not been accompanied by public discussion concerning the roles of these organizations and their relations with the powers. Nor were they accompanied by the development of a clear government policy regarding their place and roles in society, in relationship with government authorities. Furthermore, in recent years, the public image of Third Sector organizations has been harmed, particularly in the case of Amutot, creating a problematic and sometimes negative image.

The committee suggested that existing policy in this sphere is the outcome of a historical development characterized by a range of illogical internal arrangements. Some of these arrangements were created for a specific organization or group of organizations; others, created by one ministry, were not valid for other ministries; some of them are not updated and are even contradictory. Hence the need arose for a renewed examination of the existing arrangements and for the shaping of proposals to correct the prevailing situation.

Therefore, it was decided to focus on eight central topics concerning the policy for Third Sector organizations:

1. Comprehensive governmental policy towards Third Sector organizations, expressed in the understanding of these organizations, their activities, roles, and contributions.
2. The government's policy of allocations to Third Sector organizations: direct support (including contracts for purchase of services from third sector organizations and grants) and indirect support (including tax concessions for Third Sector organizations).
3. The legal framework for the existence and activities of Third Sector organizations in Israel, and mainly the supervision and control of them by government and other elements.
4. The activity of foundations and philanthropy in Israel.
5. The involvement of the business sector in Third Sector activities.
6. Self-regulation of Third Sector.
7. Organizations for social charge.
8. Third Sector organizations among the Arab population in Israel.

The report is divided into two parts. The first presents background data on Third Sector organizations in Israel, such as: The economic structure of the sector, its financial sources and scope of employment; facts and figures about associations and organizations in the sector, their areas of activity, roles, and operations, which provide a basis for the report's conclusions and recommendations. The second includes a list of recommendations for policy formulation in this domain.

The main recommendation of the report is to immediately set in motion a process for the development of a policy toward the Third Sector—a policy that will include government recognition of the unique contribution of Third Sector organizations to society and the economy in Israel.

This recognition will be based on the distinction between the different patterns of activity of the government sector, the business sector, and the Third Sector; on the importance of their mutual relations in achieving their common social and economic goals; and on the government's willingness to declare that the Third Sector organizations possess unique traits and characteristics that must be protected and nurtured. The committee believed that this policy must include a government statement of intent to rectify the mutual relations between government authorities and the Third Sector on the basis of a clear, transparent, consistent, and declared policy—a policy that will not in any way damage the independence of the Third Sector organizations.

In addition to the declarative aspect, needed to provide the Third Sector as a concept formal recognition, specific recommendations were made for

THE EVOLUTION OF THE ISRAELI THIRD SECTOR 27

particular aspects of the Third Sector listed above, such as the legislation of a law to enable the establishment of philanthropic foundations, the issue of self-regulation etc. (see Galnoor et al., 2003).

The report received a lot of coverage in the media and was officially presented (in 2003) to the state president.

6.3   *The Round Tables Project*

One of the recommendations of the Galnoor Committee was to enhance the dialog between the Third Sector and the two other sectors—the business and public sectors. This was implemented in the form of round tables that included representatives from the three sectors, which discuss issues that require policy development. The "Round Tables Project" consisted of four such tables on different issues.

Almog-Bar (2016) describes the process as follows:

> These first discussions were characterized by mutual suspicion. One of the participants from the Ministry described the main goal of this dialogue as a need "to learn how to deal with this monster." Some of the discussants portrayed the nonprofit sector as a threat to the identity of the Ministry, and expressed a feeling that it was the one setting the agenda. Some of the NPO participants noted that the discussion was too narrowly focused on the weakness of the Ministry within the Israeli government and generally in Israeli society, and that nonprofit organizations and their operations were discussed to a lesser extent. However, as a result of the discussions addressing the subjects of the elderly and Insights from the Israeli case 243 people with disabilities, the elderly and rehabilitation branches made some important changes towards nonprofit organizations, including their incorporation in policy discussions, processes of knowledge accumulation, and supervision. In addition, following these activities, a number of agreements between the Ministry and nonprofit organizations were developed and signed between the local authority and the NPOs active at the local government level. (pp. 243–244)

6.4   *The Aridor Committee*

In light of these developments, the government realized the need to intervene in the newly discovered field of activity and formed its own committee to review policy toward the Third Sector. The committee was established in 2004, and the chair of the committee was the former Minister of Finance, Yoram Aridor.

The main recommendations of the committee that were determined in 2006 were (Almog-Bar, 2016, p. 244):

1. Drafting of a partnership agreement between government and the non-profit sector.
2. Creating a central database in the register of associations.
3. Governmental support to nonprofit organizations should not exceed 60 percent of the organizations' operating budget. According to the committee, more support would turn the association in facto into a governmental unit.
4. Reducing the taxation of charities, and higher tax concessions for donations.
5. Broadening governmental inspection and supervision of nonprofits, and creating a coordination mechanism between the different governmental supervising authorities.

The establishment of the Aridor Committee by the government was an attempt to control the policy processes pertaining to the Third Sector in light of it taking a more independent stance on a variety of issues. Interestingly, the measures recommended by the Aridor Committee included the development of a database, which at that time seemed already very necessary, as data on nonprofit organizations was dispersed in different public agencies and was not synchronized.

6.5 *The Lebanon War*

The Second Lebanon War was fought between Israel and Hezbollah in the summer of 2006 in Lebanon and Northern Israel. For Israelis who lived in the northern region it meant massive bombing of towns and cities. In light of a dysfunction of government agencies to assist the civilian population, there was a comprehensive civil society mobilization to help those left in the north and the hundreds of thousands who sought refuge outside the missile range towards the center or the south of Israel. This rapid and extensive civilian mobilization stood out especially in the face of the helplessness of the government and local authorities in assisting the residents. The reality of the war emphasized the problematic nature of relations between the Third Sector and the government, and raised once more the need for a clear division of labor between the public and Third Sector, in times of crisis but also in normal times. Civilian mobilization to help northern localities on the one hand and public criticism of government dysfunction in this area on the other mark the war as a turning point in this issue of relations between the state and the Third Sector.

During the second week of the war, when the reality described above began to become clear, Katz et al. (2007) documented the behavior of the organizations during the hostilities. They found that 43 percent of the public donated money or equipment and food for the residents of the north, and 11 percent of the public volunteered to help the victims of the war in the north. In addition, 25 percent of households reported hosting families from the north (although most hosted relatives and friends, and only a fifth of them hosted foreigners). Business organizations and Third Sector organizations played a key role in mediating between donors, volunteers, and hosts and needy northerners. Half of the volunteers did so through an organization—a higher rate than that recorded in the survey of patterns of donation and volunteering among the public in Israel in 1997. In emergency situations, it appears, there is a greater need for the mediation of the organizations. This finding suggests that under war circumstances the role of Third Sector organizations in supporting and guiding the philanthropic behavior of the public has expanded. While Israeli citizens believe that meeting social needs in times of crisis is the duty of the government, however, in this war these were mainly met by Third Sector organizations and civilians.

The most obvious and prominent feature of the conduct of the organizations that the authors interviewed was a rapid and even immediate change in their activities, and their adaptation to the new circumstances and needs that arose following the bombings in the north.

The organizations' assessment of their own performance and the performance of other Third Sector organizations during the war was generally high. The assessment that was heard most of all, however, was that despite the enormous effort invested and the expansion of the activity to an unprecedented scale, the needs were far greater than the capabilities of their organizations or Third Sector organizations in general. Another explanation for the difficulty in fully responding to the needs of the residents stems from government's failure to coordinate information and assistance actions.

Following the Lebanon War, in 2008 the government published a report—"The Government of Israel, Civil Society, and the Business Community: Partnership, Empowerment, and Transparency" (Prime Minister's Office, 2008). The document focuses on the relationships between the societal sectors and states three main goals:

> (1) Establishing a relationship and strengthening the collaboration between the sectors, to the extent which they desire, while maintain the partners' independence; (2) increasing the integration of civil society organizations in the operation of social services, while encouraging discourse with them prior to making political decisions; (3) encouraging processes that contribute to empowerment, professionalization,

supervision and transparency in civil society, while implementing similar standards in the government and the business sector for working within this framework. (p. 18)

Thus, as in other domains, a crisis situation hastens processes that without it could have taken much longer.

6.6   *In the Aftermath of the 2008 Economic Crisis*

Whereas the "Round Tables Project" became permanent, it had to deal with a set of new problems in light of the 2008/09 economic crisis. Although Israel was not seriously affected economically by the 2008 crisis, it brought about two major implications for the Third Sector: (1) In light of a slow-down in philanthropic donations from abroad, the need to find new sources of funding necessitated a rise in the interest in social enterprises and other self-generated income sources by Third Sector organizations; (2) As in other countries, in 2011 a massive series of street demonstrations shook Israel with the slogan of a demand for social justice. The background was a growing gap between different factions in society. Israel, the Startup Nation, has emerged as a country with significant gaps between the rich and the poor and a system that encourages the few and neglects the many.

The list of issues discussed by the Round Tables reflects these changes:

1. Tax policy.
2. Volunteer activities.
3. Social enterprise—definition and policy. Following the economic crisis of 2008, which affected the sector significantly as donations from abroad began to dwindle (Katz & Yogev, 2010) and led to a process by which the sector began to carry out self-generated income activities (Gidron & Abbou, 2012).
4. Governmental support in financial crisis.
5. Transparency—establishment of GuideStar website.
6. Partnership in programs in education system (https://sheatufim.org.il/en/subject/cross-sector-dialog/prime-ministers-office).

7   Philanthropy

In Judaism, philanthropy is evident in charitable institutions, charitable giving, and mutual responsibility (Rozenhek & Silber, 2000). This characteristic of donation has deep roots in the Jewish tradition. The commandment of giving charity is a central one in the Bible. In the book of Deuteronomy, it is written "Open your hand to your brother and to the poor in your land." Throughout history this translated to supporting charitable institutions in the various Jewish communities. While giving to charity was expected of every Jew, the wealthy had of course a higher level of expectation.

Examples of this can be found in the activities of Jewish wealthy persons throughout the world, who worked to create community buildings and institutions, invested in real estate for the benefit of the community, and developed capital funds. Well-known examples in the modern era are the Rothschild family, Moses Montefiore, Baron Hirsch, and many more (Shimoni, 2008).

When it comes to philanthropy in Israel, the data shows that giving is relatively common among Israelis (Drezner et al., 2017; Haski-Leventhal, Yogev-Keren, & Katz, 2011; Katz & Greenspan, 2015; Katz, Levinson, & Gidron, 2007).

In the last few decades, philanthropy in Israeli society has shifted from a traditional philanthropy of charitable institutions to a new philanthropy (Schmid, 2011). The traditional philanthropy is perceived as "romantic," Zionistic, and nationalistic. The new philanthropy is based on principles of profit management (Shimoni, 2008; Silber, 2008). The new philanthropy includes wealthy people who have made their fortunes in high-tech and advanced industries (Schmid & Rudich-Cohn, 2012).

Katz, Levinson, and Gidron (2007) studied the issue of patterns of giving and volunteering following the Second Lebanon War and great assistance provided by Third Sector organizations, individual volunteers, and donors of all kinds to the civilian population in the north of the country. The study showed impressive roots of philanthropy in Israel: 44 percent of the total adult Jewish population is involved in volunteering, 19 percent of the respondents donate their time in a formal framework (within organizations), and 33 percent volunteer in an informal channel (directly with individuals and families). 7 percent of volunteers do so in both a formal and informal setting. 83 percent of the adult Jewish population donate, 72 percent of the respondents donate in a formal channel, 42 percent donate informally, and 30 percent of the population are active in both channels. The average contribution to organizations was NIS 750 per household per year.

Shimoni (2008), among his other findings, analyzed the motivations of large-scale philanthropy in Israel for donation and identified five main motives: (1) Collective and patriotic identification; (2) business taxation and positioning; (3) a desire to return to society in which they acquired their training and accumulated their wealth; (4) peer pressure in the informal social environment and an attempt to emulate them; and (5) the search for meaning and inner satisfaction.

In another study on philanthropic behavior of Israelis, Haski-Leventhal, Yogev-Keren, and Katz (2011) used a survey of 1,538 households. They found the following demographic characteristics of Israeli philanthropy: Men are more likely than women to volunteer and donate organs, but women are slightly more likely than men to donate. A positive relationship was found between income level and level of education: The richer and more educated people are more willing to volunteer and contribute, especially on the formal level, and donate organs. While married people exhibited both the highest volunteer rates and the contribution rate, divorced persons show the lowest volunteer rates and singles show the lowest contribution rates. In addition, they found that total volunteer rates and donations rates, both formal and informal, show an upward trend over the years (2006–08).

Schmid and Rudich-Cohn (2012) interviewed seventy-nine elite philanthropists. They found the average percentage of donations out of the philanthropists' total earnings was not lower than the percentage found among philanthropists in other Western countries.

Drezner and colleagues (2017) also examined the attitudes toward giving and how different factors and considerations guide household giving. Their sample included Jewish and Arab Israeli adults. They showed that there is a relatively positive attitude toward giving among respondents, and correlation between the level of trust in the nonprofit sector and the tendency to engage in philanthropy. Respondents reported that the most common means for donating were giving to beggars on the street, through tzedakah boxes, and at supermarkets or stores. They suggested that most individual and household giving in Israel is spontaneous and less strategic. In addition, they showed that giving is relatively common among Israelis (61 percent reported giving in the past year) and is more likely to be carried out by Jewish respondents, respondents with an academic degree, and those with higher level of income. They found that there are three preferred charitable beneficiaries: health, welfare, and religious organizations.

In the studies mentioned earlier (Drezner et al., 2017; Haski-Leventhal, Yogev-Keren, & Katz, 2011; Schmid & Rudich-Cohn, 2012), the data was collected by interviews, surveys, and questionnaires. A recent work by Berrebi and Yonah (2017) used unique data based on tax credits. The information was compiled from two sources—the Israel Tax Authority and the Central Bureau of Statistics Population Registry. They reported that female-headed households tended to be more generous in terms of donation as a percent of income. However, male-headed households contribute higher amounts on average. In addition, they found that new immigrant philanthropists contribute significantly higher amounts than their Israeli-born counterparts and long-time residents. With each additional year of residence in Israel, assimilating and integrating into its society, giving generosity decreases, converging with the level of Israeli-born donors. Finally, they reported that philanthropists originating from the United States and Western Europe contribute the highest

THE EVOLUTION OF THE ISRAELI THIRD SECTOR   33

amounts and are found to be the most generous donors compared to those originating from Asia, Africa, and Eastern Europe.

7.1 *Donations: Current Data*

Associations raise and receive donations from individuals, businesses, and foundations from Israel and abroad. In 2018, donations of NIS 12.3 billion were received from Israel and NIS 8.4 billion from abroad (for more details, see Appendix III).

In a report to the Registrar of Associations, the associations must report any large donation equal to or above NIS 100,000. In 2018, out of a total of NIS 20.7 billion that was received by associations from donations, NIS 9.8 billion was received from large donations. 4,989 large donations from Israel equaled NIS 3.2 billion and another 5,008 large donations from abroad totaled NIS 6.6 billion (for more details, see Appendix III).

In 2018, 43 percent of all large donations from abroad were received from donations above of NIS 10 million each. This compares with 24 percent of the large donations from Israel.

3,867 large donations from Israel and 3,256 large donations from abroad were received from donations between NIS 100,000–500,000 each (more than two-thirds of the number of large donations). At the same time, the total amount of these donations constituted 24 percent and 11 percent of the total large donations from Israel and abroad, respectively.

Income from donations in a small association amounted to an average of NIS 81,000, while in a medium-sized association, the average was NIS 937,000, and in a large association it stood at NIS 8 million.

Examining the sources of funding among each group of associations indicates differences between groups, so that on average, in small associations, 69 percent of the revenues were received from donations and 7 percent were received from the state. Meanwhile in large associations, on average 28 percent of the income was received from donations and 42 percent was received from the state.

8 Philanthropy and Civil Society in the Arab-Palestinian Society

The majority of the Arab population is Muslim, and the rest is Christian and Druze. All three religions emphasize the importance of helping others. In Islam, "zakat," helping others (especially orphans, widows, migrants, and poor people), is one of the five most sacred religious commandments that every Muslim has to fulfill.

The research on philanthropy patterns in the Arab-Palestinian society was introduced in 1993 by Neu, who examined ninety-six nonprofit Arab organizations in Israel (Neu, 1993). It continued with the studies by the Israeli Center for Third Sector Research (Gidron, 1997; Shay et al., 1999). A comprehensive study has been undertaken by Zeidan and Ghanem (2000), who examined volunteer work in Arab-Palestinian society, and the donations made to it. Zeidan (2005) expanded his research focusing on the years 2001–02. In addition, Schneider and Shoham (2017) recently published a report focusing on the development of philanthropy since Zeidan's paper, and Jamal (2017) published the book *Arab Civil Society in Israel*, focusing on the changing processes in Arab-Palestinian Society.

Zeidan and Ghanem (2000) describe four main factors that explain the development of the Third Sector in Arab-Palestinian society in Israel as follows: (1) An alternative to state organizations; (2) a source of employment and livelihood; (3) receiving approval by the Registrar of Amutot (associations); and (4) the strengthening of the religious factor.

Jamal (2017) summarized external and internal factors affecting the development of civil society within the Arab-Palestinian society in Israel. Examples for internal factors include the weakening of the Arab parties, the lack of social influence of Arab local leaders, the rise in education, number of academics, an increase in the political awareness of Arab-Palestinian citizens in Israel, involvement of young people in social initiatives, and the success of Arab-Palestinian social organizations in initiating social change. Examples for external factors included the social and economic inequality experienced by Arab-Palestinians in Israeli society, gaps in work integration, and the limited influence of Arab parties in the Knesset.

Jamal and colleagues (2019) published status of Arab-Palestinian organizations in the civil society of Israel (see Appendix IV). A comparison between Arab and Jewish organizational data shows that there is a large gap between them. The numbers of registered Jewish and Arab organizations are 39,819 and 3,895 respectively, which means that the number of associations in relation to population is 0.006 and 0.003 respectively. Also, the average number of employees and volunteers in Jewish organizations is larger: 82.5 employees in Jewish associations as compared to 38.5 in Arab associations and 147.6 volunteers in Jewish associations as compared to 19.6 in Arab associations.

9 Social Entrepreneurship and Social Enterprises

Israel was coined as the "Startup Nation" (Senor & Singer, 2009) as it developed, during the 1990s, a very advanced high-tech industry based on the creativity of entrepreneurs. That spirit could also be found among social entrepreneurs. Starting in the 1990s, a trend to develop business arms within nonprofit organizations, which could generate income from commercial activities, became evident (Mano, 2010). In a parallel step, social enterprises began to appear.

Social enterprises have been defined by the EMES Network as "organizations with an explicit aim to benefit the community, initiated by a group of citizens and in which the material interest of capital investors is subject to limits. Social enterprises also place a high value on their autonomy and on economic risk-taking related to ongoing socio-economic activity" (Defourny & Nyssens, 2006, p. 5).

The International Comparison of Social Enterprise Models (ICSEM) Project, was conducted by Jacques Defourny and Marthe Nyssens in 2013 in order to identify social enterprises models existing in fifty countries—including Israel. The researchers identified five models of social enterprises based primarily on their modes of incorporation: (1) Associations or Public Benefit Corporations; (2) business organizations or limited liability companies; (3) cooperatives; (4) public authorities—municipal or governmental; and (5) financial enterprises. The findings focus on three main aspects of the enterprises: the economic activity, the social goal, and the governance structure. The researchers concluded that the field is in its infancy and although it had been able to demonstrate some impressive successful ventures, it had not yet developed a clear and stable ecosystem to enable it to thrive. It seems that the hybrid structure of social enterprises poses difficulties for policy-makers both within the business sector and in the Third Sector (Abbou et al., 2017; Gidron et al., 2017).

10   Research, Databases, Journals, and Education Centers

The development of the Third Sector internationally, brought about a development of Third Sector research centers, some of which were engaged not only in research but in developing new databases, new journals, and educational programs were instigated by the universities. The centers in Israel can be divided into two types: Those whose main focus is the Third Sector and related concepts (two centers) and others that study the Third Sector among other topics (six centers). There are five main sources of information regarding the Third Sector in Israel: The National Bureau of Statistic (NBS), the GuideStar website, Social Map, Ruach Tova, and Midot. There are several programs in Israel that focus on nonprofit organizations, and there are two kinds of journals that discuss the Third Sector in Hebrew: specific and general. *Civil Society and the Third Sector in Israel* was the only one solely devoted to this topic. The rest are more general journals, publishing occasional articles on the Third Sector (for more details, see Appendix v).

11   Conclusions

The story of the evolution of the Third Sector and its conceptualization in Israel, which led into the formulation of policy and practice, is not necessarily different from that of other countries, where the idea that voluntary organizations, citizens' groups, and other such formations belong to a unique *sector* was a total novelty. This development, accentuated in the 1990s by the fall of the Soviet Bloc on the one hand and the enactment of policies of privatization on the other, created the background forces for a different conceptualization of society, which up until then was perceived as consisting of two sectors: The business and the public. The idea that all those diverse entities that are neither public nor business belong to a sector, which has unique characteristics and unique societal roles, was clearly a novel one then and was not easily digested by policy-makers or the public—as well as skeptics in academia— in most countries. A glance at the reality of this phenomenon in Israel some three decades later clearly demonstrates that a very long path has been traveled and the concept of a Third Sector is no longer questioned. A whole variety of institutions, structures, frameworks, educational programs, policy formulations, and more exist around it. In Israel, the building of such an infrastructure clearly finds its origin in academia.

The origins of the Third Sector in Israel can be found in the Jewish tradition of tzedaka, which compels every member of the community to contribute to the needy as well as in the web of communal organizations, which served as an infrastructure of the Jewish communities in the diaspora. This basic tradition continued in a different configuration during the pre-state era in Israel. In Islam, the commandment of zakat has a similar centrality and significance to tzedaka. The formation of the state in 1948 changed that reality and with "statism" Israel experienced a centralistic corporatist system, which did not rely on citizens' involvement. That reality changed once more starting in the 1980s and opened up the economy as well as civil society to a pluralistic approach with a multitude of actors, ideologies, and funding sources. The idea of a *Third* Sector was imported from abroad, and it took some time for it to catch on, but once data and knowledge from the academic centers on the sector was forthcoming, policy-makers and practitioners could not ignore it and structures and frameworks were built to relate to it.

The fact that during this period rich data was collected on the Third Sector enabled academics to analyze it within different theories; prominent among those are the social origins theory and the roles theory. The former enables us to identify the specific forces in society that impacted the Third Sector during different eras. The latter does that regarding the roles Third Sector organizations filled at different eras.

At the beginning of the third decade of the third millennium, the Third Sector in Israel has an impressive presence in society: It features in the provision of a variety of services in a system of contracts with the state and at the same time it is a framework for different populations to organize within civil society, address their problems, and promote their interests. The sector's diverse and fragile funding sources (in light of frequent emergencies of different types), prevent a stable existence among many organizations, but it is inconceivable to view Israeli society today without its rich and diverse web of Third Sector organizations. This, among other factors, has to do with the "discovery" by Israelis of philanthropy. Whereas in the past, philanthropy for Israel was perceived by Israelis as a domain in which Jews in the US or Europe were engaged in as a form of identification with their brethren in Israel, recent decades have seen a change, and the proportion of Israelis who donate (and volunteer) is rising. Nevertheless, because of the tradition by Jews to support those who live in the Holy Land, Israel is probably the largest *importer* of philanthropic funds per capita.

Finally, if one looks to the future, a major development that is already impacting the Third Sector is the development of social enterprises and other frameworks that combine business and commercial activity with social objectives. While obviously not all social causes can be commercialized, the idea that it is not impossible to generate such hybrid frameworks creates a new mindset in the Third Sector, which is likely to present itself more forcefully in the coming decade.

Appendix 1: The Economic Dimension

Out of the total revenue of the state, which includes NIS 38.7 billion, 57 percent of the revenue was received by education and research associations, 14 percent by culture, sports and leisure, 9 percent by welfare services, 6 percent by philanthropy and volunteering, 5 percent by religion, 2 percent by housing and development, 0.9 percent by advocacy, 0.3 percent by professional unions, 0.1 percent by environment, and 0.001 percent by international activity associations.

Out of the total revenue from donations from Israel, which includes NIS 12.3 billion, 24 percent of the revenue was received by religion associations, 23 percent by education and research, 17 percent by welfare services, 15 percent by culture, sports, and leisure, 8 percent by health, 6 percent by philanthropy and volunteering, 4 percent by advocacy, 2 percent by housing and development, 0.6 percent by environment, 0.4 percent by professional unions, and 0.03 percent by international activity associations.

Out of the total revenue from donations from abroad, which includes NIS 8.4 billion, 27 percent of the revenue was received by philanthropy and volunteering associations, 18 percent by education and research, 17 percent by religion, 17 percent by welfare services, 10 percent by culture, sports, and leisure, 5 percent by health, 3 percent by advocacy, 2 percent by housing and development, 0.2 percent by professional unions, 0.2 percent by international activity, and 0.1 percent by environmental associations.

The revenues distribution: 10 percent of the associations are associations with the highest income—they hold 84 percent of the income of all the associations. Meanwhile, 90 percent of the other associations hold 16 percent of the total income.

In 2018, the average income of a small association was NIS 120,000, the average income of a medium-sized association was NIS 2 million, and the average income of a large association was NIS 48 million. Among the large associations the variance of income is the greatest, so there are few large associations that pull the average upwards. The income in each half of the large associations was 17 million at most.

Revenues from the state in a small association amounted to an average of NIS 11,000, in a medium-sized association NIS 599,000, and in a large association NIS 20 million. Revenues from the sale of services to private parties in a small association amounted to an average of NIS 29,000, in a medium-sized association it was NIS 561,000, and in a large association NIS 19 million on average.

Appendix 11: Civil Society and Social Movements

(a) *Supports under Article 3A*

According to data from the Accountant General's Division in the Ministry of Finance, the support under Article 3A, which was transferred to nonprofit organizations in 2018 amounted to NIS 2.8 billion (Israel NPOs Yearbook, 2020). These supports have been received by a total of 2,480 nonprofit organizations. 44 percent of these worked in the field of religion, 27 percent in culture, sports, and leisure, 16 percent in education and research, and the remaining 13 percent were associations from the other eight areas of activity. Respectively, 42 percent of the total support went to religious associations, 35 percent to culture, sports, and leisure, 16 percent to education and research, and the remaining 7 percent to associations from other fields (figure 1).

In 2018, the supports under Article 3A, according to the Accountant General's data, in the amount of NIS 2.8 billion, constitute 7 percent of the total funds received by nonprofit organizations from the state (total amount of NIS 38 billion).

For example, the 1,095 associations in the field of religion that received support under Article 3A represent 59 percent of all associations in the field of religion that reported any income from the state, and the total support under Article 3A received from these associations constitutes 61 percent of total state revenue received. The 390 education and research associations that received support under Article 3A represent 22 percent of education and research associations that reported income from the state, and the total support under Section 3A that received constitutes only

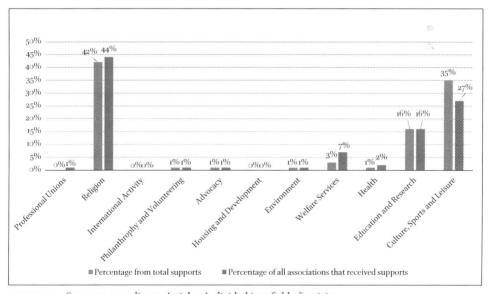

FIGURE 1   Supports according to Article 3A, divided into field of activity

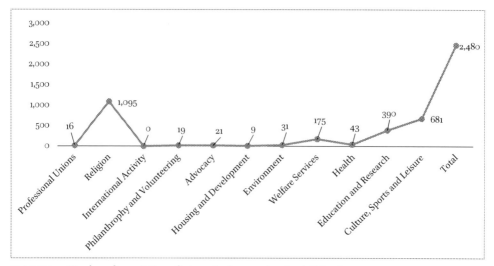

FIGURE 2   Number of associations that received support under Article 3A

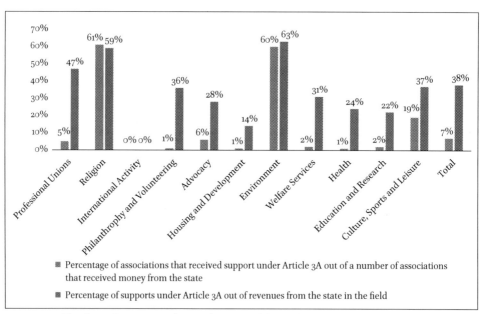

■ Percentage of associations that received support under Article 3A out of a number of associations that received money from the state
■ Percentage of supports under Article 3A out of revenues from the state in the field

FIGURE 3   The share of supports under Article 3A out of the total revenues from the state, by field of activity

2 percent of the income of education and research associations from the state (Israel NPOs Yearbook, 2020) (figure 2 & figure 3).

(b) Grants from Social Security Funds

According to data from the Social Security Funds, in 2018 the total grants transferred to nonprofit organizations amounted to NIS 121 million. These grants were received by 257 nonprofit organizations. According to the nonprofit organizations' classification of activities, 33 percent were in education and research, 16 percent in health, 15 percent in culture, sports, and leisure, and the remaining 8 percent were associations from the other seven areas of activity. 39 percent of the total grants went to welfare services associations, 25 percent to health, 17 percent to education and research, and the remaining 19 percent of the grants went to associations from other fields (Israel NPOs Yearbook, 2020) (figure 4 & figure 5).

(c) Grants from a Foreign Political Entity

Associations must report grants and donations received from a foreign political entity. In 2018 a small number of nonprofit organizations (152) received grants from a foreign political entity, amounting to NIS 489 million. The field of philanthropy and volunteering is prominent compared to the other fields, with grants from a foreign political entity totaling NIS 348 million received from three nonprofit organizations in the field.

The bulk of the total grants was received by the Holocaust Victims' Welfare Fund (NIS 346 million), which is in fact 99 percent of the total grants in the field and 71 percent of the total grants. Most of the associations that report grants from foreign

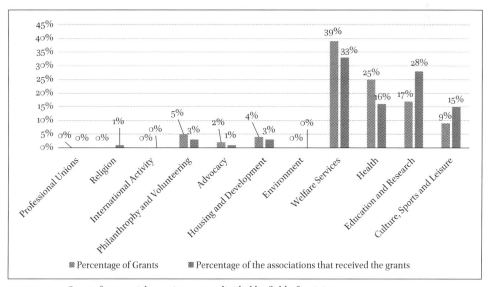

FIGURE 4 Grants from social security grants, divided by field of activity

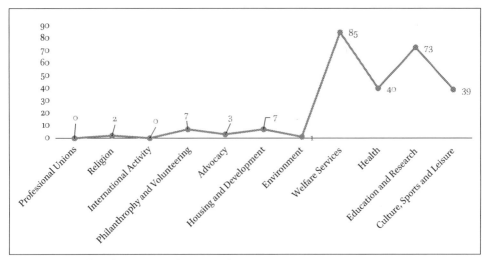

FIGURE 5   Number of associations that received grants

political entities are concentrated in the fields of education and research, culture, sports, and leisure, and advocacy (44, 38, and 34 associations respectively). At the same time, 12 percent of the associations in the field of advocacy received grants from a foreign political entity, compared with a maximum of 8 percent of the associations in all other areas (Israel NPOs Yearbook, 2020) (figure 6 & figure 7).

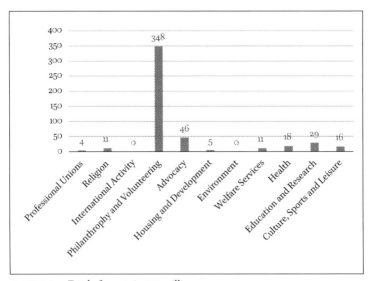

FIGURE 6   Total of grants in NIS millions

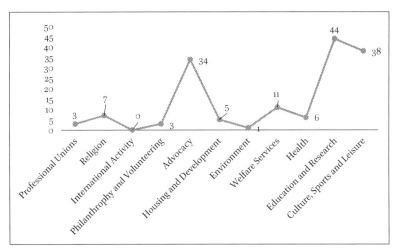

FIGURE 7   Number of associations that received grants from foreign political entity

(d)   Social Movement Organizations

Women. There are over fifty registered women's organizations, the majority of which are devoted to providing solutions to problems women face, such as preschool daycare, assistance for single mothers, and legal counseling. Other organizations have a more general agenda focused on issues such as peace, security, and social welfare (Himeyn Raisch, 2008). Examples of organizations include: The Women's Lobby in Israel, Female Spirit—economic independence for women affected by violence, and Salit—assistance to women in the prostitution circle. A famous women's group was Four Mothers, a protest group that struggled in the late 1990s to get the Israeli government to withdraw from Lebanon in light of the high price the country paid in killed and wounded soldiers and the uselessness of the army staying there. The group is credited for finally convincing the government (through a series of constant demonstrations, vigils, and public pressure), to end the Lebanon saga in the year 2000.

Arab-Palestinians. Some of the Arab-Palestinian community organizations' focus on inequality in general. The most prominent is Adallah ("justice" in Arabic), which presents itself as an independent human rights organization and a legal center (see Appendix IV). A comprehensive list of all Arab civil society organizations in Israel can be found at the OnePlace website (https://in-oneplace.net/civil_society_list/).

In addition to Arab-Palestinian organizations fighting for equality and serving their community, there are also Jewish-Arab organizations with the same goals. Prominent among these is Sikkuy.

LGBTQ. The Aguda, the Association for LGBTQ Equality in Israel was founded in 1975. Since its establishment, the Aguda has striven to improve the LGBT community's standing in Israel to achieve equal rights and security. The Aguda's URL is https://www.lgbt.org.il/english.

The Haredi Ultra-Orthodox community. This community, which tries to preserve its unique identity and interact with the rest of society only when necessary, is known for its web of organizations providing solutions for their specific needs in different fields, such as health, education, employment, family violence, abuse of men and women, children with disabilities, and legal aid. Information regarding such organizations can be found in Kol Zchut (https://www.kolzchut.org.il/).

Israelis of Ethiopian descent. The Israeli Association of Ethiopian Jews (IAEJ) is the major organization representing this population. Founded in 1993, it advances equitable policies to close gaps, change prevailing attitudes, and improve the quality of life of Israelis of Ethiopian descent on every level: with the community, municipal and state decision-makers, the media, and civil society. See https://www.iaej.co.il/language/en/association-of-ethiopian-jews/.

Appendix III: Philanthropy

(a) *Israel Donations*

In 2018 (Israel NPOs Yearbook, 2020), philanthropy and volunteer associations received an average of NIS 2.8 million in donations from Israel (including grants from foundations). The advocacy association received an average of NIS 2 million and the health association received an average of NIS 1.6 million. This is compared to NIS 177,000 and NIS 113,000 which were received on average by the professional unions and the international activity associations respectively.

At the same time, the highest median values are in the areas of welfare services and religion. So, in half of the welfare services organizations, the donations from Israel amounted to at least NIS 144,000, and in half of the religious organizations, they amounted to at least NIS 128,000. Half of the housing and development associations and professional unions did not receive any donations from Israel (Israel NPOs Yearbook, 2020) (figure 8 & figure 9).

There is also a difference in the concentration of donations and in the ceiling of donations. More than 80 percent of the donations that were received by philanthropy and volunteering associations were concentrated in 5 percent of the organizations in the field, and the highest donation in the field was NIS 149 million. While, in the field of religion, the donations are much more distributed, so that 80 percent of the donations in Israel to religious nonprofit organizations were received in 20 percent of the nonprofit organizations in the field, and the highest donation in the field was NIS 49 million (Israel NPOs Yearbook, 2020).

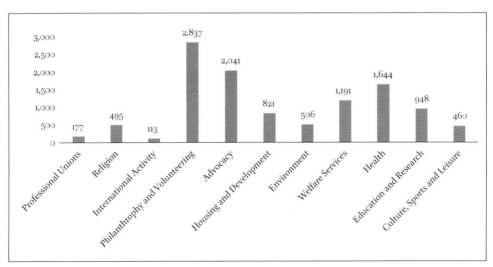

FIGURE 8   Average of donations from Israel in 2018 (in thousands), by field of activity

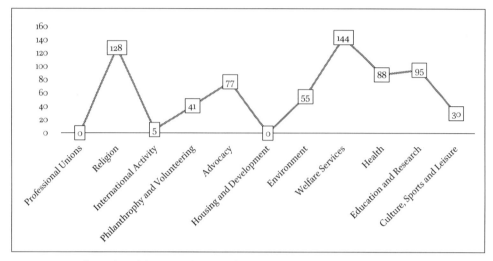

FIGURE 9   Median value of donations from Israel in 2018 (in thousands), by field of activity

(b)   *Donations from Abroad*

In 2018 (Israel NPOs Yearbook, 2020), philanthropy and volunteer associations received donations from abroad in the amount of NIS 8 million. In the other areas, an association received an average of donations from abroad in the range of NIS 1.1 million (in advocacy) and NIS 47,000 (in the environmental field).

In all areas, without exception, at least half of the associations did not receive any donations from abroad in 2018. In fact, only 22 percent from the associations reported donations from abroad (figure 10 & figure 11).

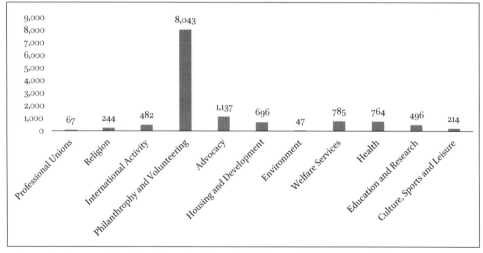

FIGURE 10   Average of donations from Israel in 2018 (in thousands), by field of activity

THE EVOLUTION OF THE ISRAELI THIRD SECTOR

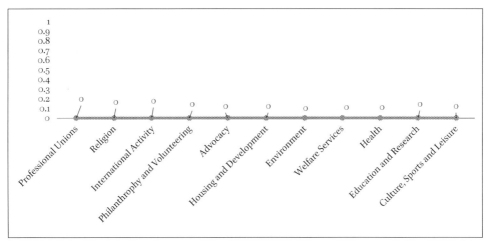

FIGURE 11   Median value of donations from abroad in 2018, by field of activity

The highest total donations from Israel and abroad is in the field of religion (NIS 4.4 billion) and of education and research (NIS 4.3 billion). These two areas are also prominent in the rate of large donations: In the field of education and research, 56 percent of all donations in the field were received from large donations (NIS 2.4 billion) and in the field of religion, 42 percent of all donations in the field were received from large donations (NIS 1.8 billion). At the same time, in the field of advocacy, the rate of large donations is the highest (69 percent), but the amount of donations is medium compared to other fields (NIS 547 million) (figure 12).

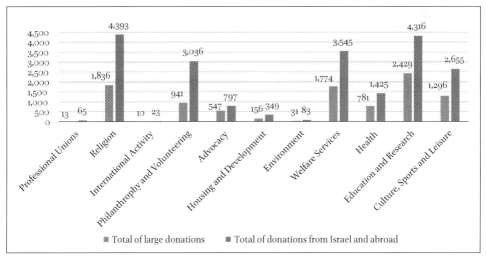

FIGURE 12   Total donations from Israel and abroad and large donations, by field of activity

(c) *Large Donations from Israel*

The fields of religion and of education and research are prominent in the number of large donations from Israel (1,336 and 1,251, respectively). In the field of education and research, the largest donations from Israel amount to NIS 839 million. In the field of religion, to the figure was NIS 581 million. In the field of profesional unions, two large donations of NIS 400,000 were received, and in the field of international activity, no

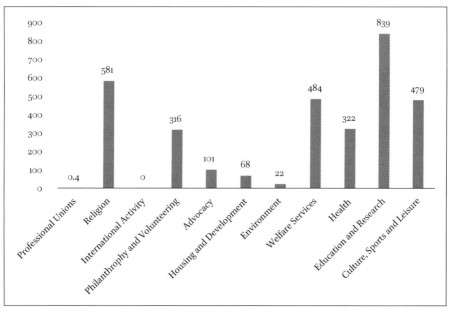

FIGURE 13   Large donations from Israel by field of activity

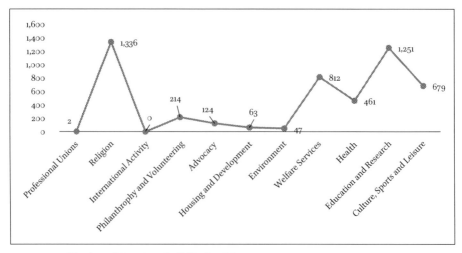

FIGURE 14   Number of donations by field of activity

large donations were received from Israel at all (Israel NPOs Yearbook, 2020) (figure 13 & figure 14).

(d)   *Large Donations from Abroad*

In terms of large donations from abroad, religion and education and research also stand out in the largest number of donations (1,514 large donations in religion and 1,274 large donations in education and research). In addition, those fields also receive the largest amount of donations: NIS 1.6 billion received for education and research associations and NIS 1.3 billion for religious associations. At the same time, the field of welfare services also stands out with large donations in the amount of NIS 1.3 billion. In the areas of professional unions and international activity, a few large donations were received at the total amount of NIS 12 million and NIS 10 million, respectively (Israel NPOs Yearbook, 2020) (figure 15 & figure 16).

(e)   *Tax Credit Certificate for Donation*

According to data from the Tax Authority, in 2018, 6,769 of the nonprofit organizations included in the yearbook 2020 (Israel NPOs Yearbook, 2020) (41 percent) had a certificate for a tax credit for a donation. The total donations from Israel (excluding donations from foundations) they received constituted 84 percent of the total donations from Israel received by all the associations. This means that 16 percent of the donations in Israel, donations in the amount of NIS 1.6 billion, were granted to nonprofit organizations without the donors being able to receive a tax benefit in return for

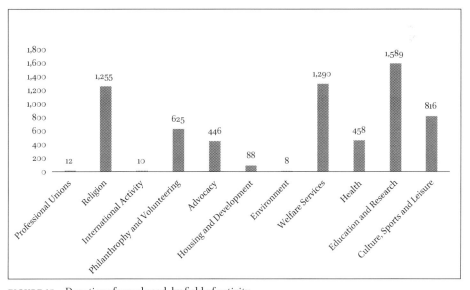

FIGURE 15   Donations from abroad, by field of activity

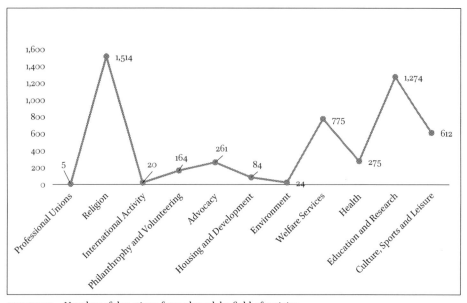

FIGURE 16   Number of donations from abroad, by field of activity

them. A maximum of 58 percent of the nonprofit organizations in each of the areas of activity had a tax credit for a donation.

In most areas, the total donations from Israel received by organizations with a certificate ranged from 76 percent to 98 percent of the total donations from Israel received by all nonprofit organizations in the field. This is with the exception of the field of professional unions, where 3 percent of associations with a tax credit certificate received 8 percent of all donations from Israel to the field, and the field of international activity where 16 percent of associations with a certificate received 58 percent of Israeli donations received in the field (figure 17 and figure 18).

(f)   *Large Donations by Size*

In 2018, at least one large donation was received in 4 percent of the small associations, in 36 percent of the medium-sized associations, and in 51 percent of the large associations. Although receiving large donations does not characterize small donations at all (since 96 percent of them did not receive any large donations), the total large donations in a small association that did receive a large donation was NIS 213,000 on average. Among 36 percent of the medium-sized associations that received a large donation, the total large donations averaged NIS 1 million per association, meanwhile,

THE EVOLUTION OF THE ISRAELI THIRD SECTOR

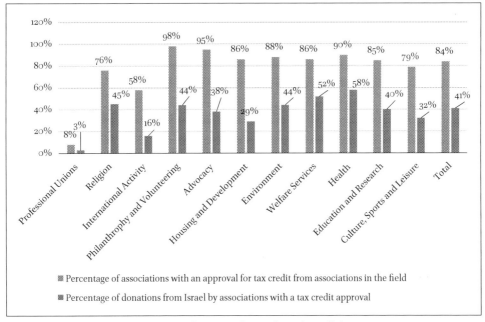

FIGURE 17   The share of associations with a tax credit certificate from all the associations

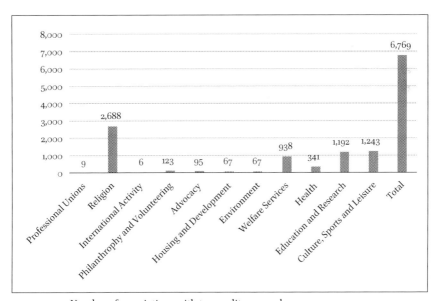

FIGURE 18   Number of associations with tax credit approval

TABLE 1 Large donations and donations from Israel with a tax credit, by size of association

% of associations that received large donation	Total of large donations on average to an association that has received at least one large donation	Number of associations by size	% of associations with tax credit certificate	% donations from Israel by associations with a tax credit certificate
4%	NIS 213,000	8,250 small associations	28%	52%
36%	NIS 1 million	6,600 meduim associations	52%	77%
51%	NIS 9 million	1,650 large associations	65%	90%

among 51 percent of the large associations that received a large donation, the total large donations averaged NIS 9 million per association (Table 1).

The three groups also differ in the percentage of associations that have a tax credit certificate. 28 percent of the small associations, 52 percent of the medium-sized associations, and 65 percent of the large associations held a tax credit approval in 2018. In addition, out of all donations from Israel received in small associations, 52 percent were received in small associations that have a tax credit approval.

As a result, 48 percent of all donations from Israel received from small associations were granted without the possibility of a tax credit; among medium-sized associations, 77 percent of donations in Israel were received by associations that had a tax credit; and aamong large associations, 90 percent of the donations in Israel were received by associations that held a tax credit (Israel NPOs Yearbook, 2020).

THE EVOLUTION OF THE ISRAELI THIRD SECTOR

Appendix IV: Arab-Palestinians in Israel Civil Society

According to Jamal et al. (2019):

The number of registered and active Arab associations[4] is 3,895 and 1,298 respectively. The branches of activities of the Arab-Palestinian in active associations are as follow: education 23 percent, sports 18 percent, welfare services 12.5 percent, religion 14.6 percent, culture and arts 12 percent, community and society 11 percent.

Only 555 associations out of 1,298, (43 percent), reported financial data. Most of the associations, 57.3 percent of all nonprofit organizations that reported the annual financial data, have an income of less than NIS 500,000. Only 17.3 percent of the nonprofit organizations that reported their annual financial data enjoy a budget higher than NIS 2 million.

(a) *Government Funding*

The percentage of Arab associations that have active contractual engagements with government ministries is very low—only twenty-two out of 1,298 active associations. The number of associations that received support under Article 3A of the Budget Basics Law is 296, which constitutes 8.22 percent of all the associations active in Arab-Palestinian society. Given their minority status and the low support from government, thirty-one civil society organizations (2.4 percent of the total number of active associations) receive funding from foreign sources (mainly Europe, Canada, and the US).

(b) *Employees and Volunteers*

365 active organizations reported employees working in their organizations. The total number of employees reported in the active Arab-Palestinian organizations was 14,055. This is an average of 38.5 employees per organization. 226 active organizations reported volunteers working in their organizations. The total number of volunteers in the active Arab organizations was 4,432 and the average was twenty volunteers per organization.

---

4 This refers to organizations of the Arab community and those serving specifically that community. There are obviously organizations that serve Israelis at large, which may have branches in Arab communities.

Appendix v: Research Centers, Databases, Education Programs, and Journals

(a) *Research Centers*

(i) The Israeli Center for Third Sector Research (ICTR) at Ben-Gurion University of the Negev

The center was established at Ben-Gurion University of the Negev in 1997 "in order to conduct and promote academic research and study civil society, the Third Sector, and related fields in Israel." The founder of the center and its director (for twelve years) was Benjamin Gidron (see https://pre.bgu.ac.il/en/fom/Ictr/Pages/default.aspx).

The center was clearly a pioneer in introducing the concept of the Third Sector in Israel. Established in 1997 as a multi- and interdisciplinary research center, funded by a grant from Atlantic Philanthropies, it engaged in a variety of activities to introduce the Third Sector concept to the Israeli research community, policy-makers, and the public at large.

The initial step ICTR took was to write the Israeli chapter in the ICNPO (Johns Hopkins Project). The ICNPO produced a number of research reports and publications on the different dimensions of the sector (Bar-Mor, 1999; Gidron, 1997, 1999; Gidron & Katz, 1998, 1999; Shay et al., 1999).

Starting in its first year, ICTR organized an annual spring conference, in which new research findings, from Israel and from abroad, were featured. Some of the major international leaders of the field at the time participated in those, such as Lester Salamon, Helmut Anheier, Dennis Young, Margaret Harris, Jeremy Kendall, Avner Ben-Ner, Joel Fleishman, and others. The conferences, many of which took place in a hotel on the Dead Sea, were attended not only by academics but by policy-makers and practitioners. The events turned out to be an excellent place for networking among participants. In those conferences scholarships were granted to MA and PhD students who studied the Third Sector and related topics in all institutions of higher education. The last conference was held in 2012.

Another major feature of ICTR was the development of the first Third Sector database. The project, initially headed by Hagai Katz, took data from different public sources, such as the Registrar of Associations, Income Tax, the State Allocations Office, and so on, each with its own system of organizing the data, and combined those into one system, which enabled researchers to explore patterns of registration, of government funding, of geographic dispersal, and much more. Given the ICNPO classification, it enabled researchers for the first time to explore the data in depth. This was the first version of the Israeli GuideStar, which was to be established about a decade later.

The role of ICTR in promoting the *formulation of policy* toward the Third Sector in forming and supporting the Galnoor Committee and its recommendations has already been discussed above.

Finally, in 2007, given the scope and importance of Third Sector research, ICTR introduced a peer-reviewed academic journal (in Hebrew). The editor was Dr. Varda Schiffer and the journal was produced for five years, finally ceasing publication for budgetary reasons.

The journal's publications were added to the list of research reports ICTR produced on a regular basis on a variety of topics:

– The analysis of the boundaries, characteristics and processes of the Third Sector (Gidron & Katz, 1998);
– The roles of the Third Sector (Gidron, Katz, & Bar, 2000; Iekowitz et al., 2002);
– The first databases (Gidron, 1999; Gidron & Alon, 2004);
– Economic data (Gidron & Katz, 1999; Katz et al., 2006; Katz & Yogev-Keren, 2013);
– Legal aspects (Bar-Mor, 1999);
– Civil society (Sharir, Heilborn, & Lazar, 2005);
– Government policy (Telias, Katan, & Gidron, 2000; Katz, Gidron, & Limor, 2009);
– ICTR's sponsorship of the Galnoor Committee (Galnoor, 2006; Galnoor et al., 2003);
– Philanthropy/patterns of giving and volunteering (Gidron, 1997, 1999; Gidron et al., 2006; Haski, Yogev-Keren, & Katz, 2011; Katz, Levinson, & Gidron, 2007; Shay et al., 1999; Silber, 2008);
– Patterns of giving and volunteering in the Arab-Palestinian society (Zeidan, 2005; Zeidan & Ghanem, 2000);
– Studies on the Ethiopian community (Belbachin, 2008);
– Organizations for social change (Kaufman & Gidron, 2006);
– Corporate social responsibility (Abbou, 2013; Raichel, Gidron, & Shani-Gamliel, 2000).

(ii)   The Center for the Study of Civil Society and Philanthropy in Israel
The center was established in 2006 at The Hebrew University of Jerusalem. It was established in partnership with JDC-Israel. The founder is Hilel Schmid and the head of the center is Michal Almog-Bar (see: https://openscholar.huji.ac.il/s-wcivilsocietyen/Publications).

The focus of the center, as the name suggests, is philanthropy and civil society. It has published a significant number of research reports to date. These include:

– Theory of philanthropy (Rudich, 2007);
– Attitudes towards philanthropy (Schmid & Rudich, 2008);
– Philanthropic foundations (Brenner et al., 2010);
– Effectiveness of philanthropy (Auerbach, 2009);
– Types of philanthropy (new, elite) (Schmid et al., 2009; Shimoni, 2008);
– Characteristics of philanthropy (Schmid, 2013);
– History of philanthropy (Haski-Leventhal & Kabalo, 2009);
– Jewish philanthropy (Levi D'Ancona, 2010; Salamon, 2008);

- Psychological effects on the motivation for philanthropic activity (Kogot & Ritov, 2010);
- The impact of funding on organization (Schmid, 2013);
- Cross sectoral partnership (Almog-Bar, Schmid, & Lachman-Lazar, 2013; Almog-Bar & Zichlinsky, 2010a; Hazan, 2009; Schmid & Almog-Bar, 2013, 2016; Schmid, Shaul Bar, & Nisisim, 2015a);
- Social change (Lazar, 2013);
- Advocacy (Fleischmann, 2009);
- Tax policy and donations (Hazan, 2010);
- Globalization of philanthropy (Schmid & Shaul-Bar Nissim, 2013);
- Welfare associations in Israel (Madhala, Almog-Bar, & Gal, 2018);
- Intergenerational transmission of philanthropic behavior (Schmid, Shaul-Bar Nissim, & Niral, 2018);
- Environmental philanthropy (Greenspan, 2014);
- Civil society in Israel (Almog-Bar & Greenspan, 2019);
- Arabs in civil society in Israel (Jamal et al., 2019);
- Volunteering and social involvement during the COVID-19 crisis in Israel (Almog-Bar & Bar, 2020).

The following research centers, focusing on diverse social sciences and economics, occasionally publish papers on the Third Sector and civil society.

(iii)   Taub Center for Social Policy Studies in Israel at Tel Aviv University

The center was established in 1982. The main publications of the Taub Center include the "State of the State Report—Society, Economy and Policy" from the Singer series, and the accompanying publication "State of the State: Charts on Society and Economy in Israel." The center also periodically publishes the Roshendler Newsletter and policy summaries, which include brief and professional analyses of current issues. The researchers, policy colleagues, and experts of the Taub Center write policy documents that are published and distributed to a wide audience in Israel and abroad (see: http://taubcenter.org.il/research/).

(iv)   The Walter Lebach Institute for Jewish-Arab Coexistence through Education

The institute was established in 2002. Its publications are related to its core interests, including psychological factors and their impact on the peace process, Third Sector activity in Israel, land policies in the Negev Desert, legal issues, the occupations and its implication on Israel society, and the dilemmas of recognition in conflicts (see: https://en-social-sciences.tau.ac.il/centers).

(v)   The Van Leer Jerusalem Institute

The institute was established in 1959. Research and public engagement take place in four thematic clusters: Sacredness, religion and secularization; globalization and sovereignty; science, technology, and civilization; and Israel in the Middle East. Alongside work in these clusters, the institute fosters a large-scale project promoting gender equality in Israel, and serves as a platform for thinking through and beyond challenges to liberal democracy in our time (see: https://www.vanleer.org.il/).

(vi)   The Knesset Research and Information Center (RIC)

RIC was established in 2000. It provides the Knesset members, committees, and government departments with data, research papers, and background studies pertaining to current debates, legislation, and relevant parliamentary activity (see: https://main .knesset.gov.il/EN/activity/Pages/MMMAbout.aspx).

(vii)   The Israel Democracy Institute (IDI)

IDI is an independent center of research and action dedicated to strengthening the foundations of Israeli democracy. The institute partners with government, policy- and decision makers, the civil service, and society, to improve the functioning of the government and its institutions, confront security threats while preserving civil liberties, and foster solidarity within Israeli society (see: https://en.idi.org.il/about/about-idi/).

(viii)   JDC Institute for Leadership and Governance

The institute is divided into three components: The Center for Public Leadership and Management, The Center for Mayors and Regional Development, and The Center for Lay Leadership and Civil Society. These work in conjunction with one another to provide networking opportunities and services to senior leaders throughout Israel (see: http://www.theinstitute.org.il/index.php?dir=site&page=content&cs=3000).

Some examples of reports published by these centers pertaining to the Third Sector and related topics include:

- Berrebi & Yonah (2017), *Philanthropy in Israel: An Updated Picture* (Taub Center);
- Jamal et al. (2019) with their examination of Arab-Palestinian civil society (Walter Lebach Institute for Jewish-Arab Coexistence through Education);
- Limor & Avishai (2013) with a study of the government—civil society organizations partnership (Van Leer Jerusalem Institute, 2020);
- Schwartz's (2009) examination of the implications of the economic crisis on the Third Sector (The Knesset Research and Information Center);
- Limor's (2010) study of civil society and the Third Sector in Israel (The Israel Democracy Institute);
- Aines, Drori, & Lester Levy's (2011) discussion of volunteer leadership (JDC Institute for Leadership and Governance).

(b)   *Databases*

(i)   The National Bureau of Statistics (NBS)

Since 1991, the NBS has systematically collected NPIS' data by using surveys and publishes reports on its website (see: https://www.cbs.gov.il), under National Accounts. According to the System of National Accounts, NPIS are defined as "legal or social entities that were established for the purpose of producing goods and services, whose status does not permit them to be a source of income, profit, or other financial gain for the units that establish, finance, or control them" (see: https://www.cbs.gov.il). Following the UN National Accounts system, the NPIS are divided into eleven fields of activity: 1) culture, recreation, and sports; 2) education and research; 3) health; 4) social services; 5) environment; 6) housing and development; 7) advocacy and politics; 8) philanthropy and voluntarism; 9) international activity; 10) religion; and 11) professional associations.

The NBS publishes the income and expenses report every two to three years. The report lists the various sources of financing of the nonprofit sector and the expenditure components, as well as the economic activity of nonprofit organizations and the number of employees and volunteers in the sector, by areas of activity. In addition, it publishes the nonprofit income survey, which presents detailed data on Israel's philanthropy, one of the sources of funding for nonprofit organizations, as part of the nonprofit's income, organized by source, destination, and donation size.

(ii)   GuideStar

GuideStar Israel is the main information website about individual nonprofit organizations in Israel. Established in 2009 it is a government project managed by the Ministry of Justice in collaboration with JDC-Israel (American-Jewish Joint Distribution Committee), and is accompanied by a public advisory committee that includes representatives of government ministries, civil society, and the business sectors (see: https://www.guidestar.org.il/home).

(iii)   Social Map

The Social Map website is an innovative project to create a first-of-its-kind database, which enables the general public to get a broad and comprehensive picture of the organizations and associations operating in Israel and the degree of involvement and government support in their activities (see: https://socialmap.org.il/).

(iv)   Ruach Tova

Ruach Tova ("good spirit" in Hebrew) is a leading organization in the field of volunteering in Israel, specializing in matching volunteers with organizations. Ruach Tova operates a unique website, which is a search engine for finding personalized volunteers. The website has information about persons/groups/organizations needing volunteers and creates a match according to their location in the country, hours when

THE EVOLUTION OF THE ISRAELI THIRD SECTOR

they want to volunteer, and the area in which they want to volunteer (see: https://www.ruachtova.org.il/organizationsindex).

(v)   Midot

Midot is a nonprofit company that strives to promote effectiveness and impact as the main criterion for social investors and for NPO leaders by rating NPOs and producing sector analysis reports.

The purpose of Midot's examinations is to evaluate NPOs' effectiveness—that is, their ability to create social value and improve the lives of their beneficiaries. To do this, Midot uses a rating methodology that was developed after an in-depth examination of the different organization evaluation methods around the world, and following conversations with organizations, donors, and experts in the Third Sector. During the rating process a range of organizational capacities are examined: The organization's planning and performance abilities, how it measures its activities and sustains processes of learning and participation, its human capital, its financial management, and more (see: http://www.midot.org.il/english-2015).

(c)   *Education Programs*

The following are several programs in Israel that focus on nonprofit organizations:

(i) University of Haifa. MBA Program in Management of Nonprofit Organizations at the Faculty of Management at the School of Business Administration (see: http://management.haifa.ac.il).

(ii) Ben-Gurion University of the Negev. MBA Program in Social Leadership at the Guilford Glazer Faculty of Business and Management (see: http://in.bgu.ac.il/).

(iii) The Hebrew University of Jerusalem. Schwartz Program, MA in Nonprofit and Community Organization Management in The Paul Baerwald School of Social Work and Social Welfare (see: https://sw.huji.ac.il).

(d)   *Journals*

(i)   Civil Society and The Third Sector in Israel

The launching of the journal *Civil Society and the Third Sector in Israel* in 2006 was a milestone in the development of those subjects in Israel. Its publication proved that there was a group of active researchers who could produce research on the topic. The issues that the journal dealt with were at the heart of social developments and the structural changes that have affected most of the democratic countries in the last decade. So, for example, the second journal published essays that dealt with internal organizational questions of sustainability and ways of mobilizing resources, and with questions that deal with the links between the organization and its clients, and with the public (Brochure, 2007).

The editor was Dr. Varda Shiffer and issues were published between 2007 and 2011. The journal had to discontinue in 2012.

The topics discussed in *Civil Society and the Third Sector in Israel* include:

- Philanthropy (Gidron, Schlanger, & Alon, 2008; Katz & Haski-Leventhal, 2008; Meslin, Rooney, & Wolf, 2008; Silber, 2008; Solek, 2010);
- Civil society (Gidron, 2007, 2011; Menuchim, 2011; Sembira & Fuchs, 2007);
- Dialogue between sectors (The Interface Round Table Staff, 2010; Tamir, 2007);
- Government support versus public support (Limor, 2008);
- Social change (Strychman & Marshud, 2007);
- Characteristics of volunteers (Jaffe, York, & Kfir, 2011);
- Management in the Third Sector (Amit & Kreindler, 2010);
- Topography of self-groups (Schusterman, 2010);
- Decision making in the elderly home care (Abbou, 2007);
- Social capital (Zichlinsky, 2010);
- Board members of NPOs (Bar-Mor & Iecovich, 2007);
- Managed giving (Haber, 2011);
- Family foundation (Sembira, 2008);
- The Third Sector during the Second Lebanon War (Katz et al., 2007);
- Social organizations (Amit, 2011; Portugaly, Miller-Danieli, 2007; Rikoula, Mano & Hareven, 2007);
- Planning and implementing mergers of third sector organizations;
- Responsibility in the age of globalization (Anheier, 2007).

(ii)   Social Security

Social Security is published three times a year, starting in 1971, by the National Insurance Institute. The journal publishes papers dealing with social policy, social security, social rights, and welfare issues. In the broad aspect, economic, political, sociological, demographic, geographical, and historical aspects are discussed, as well as education, health, and law (The National Insurance Institute, 2020).

Examples of articles published in *Social Security* which discuss the Third Sector include:

- Rewards from volunteer work and volunteer management (Gidron, 1977; Yanay-Ventura & Livena, 2010);
- Characteristics of voluntary organizations (Iekowitz & Katan, 2005; Katan, 1988);
- Civil society (Almog-Bar & Eisenstadt, 2015; Almog-Bar & Zichlinsky, 2010b; Schmid, 2015);
- The relationship between the government and associations (Auerbach, 2008);
- The impact of privatization (Zichlinsky, 2010);
- The government and philanthropic foundations (Almog-Bar & Zichlinsky, 2010b; Schmid & Shaul-Bar-Nisisim, 2015b);

THE EVOLUTION OF THE ISRAELI THIRD SECTOR   61

- Patterns of giving and volunteering (Gidron & Lazar, 1998);
- Advocacy in NPOs (Schmid, Almog-Bar, & Niral, 2008).

(iii)   Israeli Sociology

Israeli Sociology has been published twice a year since 1998. It was founded by the Department of Sociology and Anthropology at Tel Aviv University. The journal serves as a platform for local studies, yet in dialogue with a sociological scholarship around the world. It encourages a variety of theoretical and methodological approaches, in line with the heterogeneity of the discipline, and further offers a platform for debating the sociological research agenda in general and the sociological reality in Israel in particular (*Israeli Sociology*, 2020).

Examples of papers published in *Israeli Sociology* that discuss the Third Sector include Ben Eliezer's (1999) study of the civil society in Israel; Gidron, Bar, and Katz's (2002) examination of the characteristics of Israeli organized civil society; and Rosolio's (2006) analysis of the Third Sector and civil society.

(iv)   Chevra Ve'Revacha

Chevra Ve'Revhach (Society and Welfare) started publication in 1978. The aim of the journal is to expand and deepen the theoretical, research, and applied knowledge of social workers and other welfare professionals such as psychologists, criminologists, public health workers, and sociologists (*Chevra Ve'Revacha*, 2020).

Examples of papers published in *Chevra Ve'Revacha* on the Third Sector include Gidron's (1983) examination of volunteers' satisfaction in their work; Bar's (2001) study of the involvement of voluntary welfare organizations in the processes of determining welfare policy; Iekowitz's (2006) study of public management in voluntary organizations; and Livnat and Almog-Bar's (2018) analysis of the employment experience of middle managers in Third Sector organizations in Israel.

References

Abbou, I. (2007). Attitudes and decision making in the elderly home care mixed market in Israel. *Civil Society and the Third Sector in Israel, 1*(2), 75–96.

Abbou, I. (2013). *Social responsibility in business organizations—examining the relationship between core components and the scope of social responsibility and patterns of inclusion of responsibility in public firms in Israel.* Beersheba: Israeli Center for Third Sector Research, Ben-Gurion University of the Negev (in Hebrew).

Abbou, I., Gidron, B., Buber-Ben David, N., Greenberg, Y., Monnickendam-Givon, Y., & Navon, A. (2017). Social enterprise in Israel: The swinging pendulum between collectivism and individualism. *Social Enterprise Journal, 13*(4), 329–344.

Aines, G., Drori, R., & Lester Levy, M. (2011). The guide to volunteer leadership. JDC Institute for Leadership and Governance.

Almog-Bar, M. (2016). Policy initiatives towards the nonprofit sector: Insights from the Israeli case. *Nonprofit Policy Forum, 7*(2), 237–256.

Almog-Bar, M., & Bar, R. (2020). Volunteering and social involvement during the corona crisis in Israel: Information, insights and challenges. The Center for the Study of Civil Society and Philanthropy in Israel, at The Hebrew University of Jerusalem (in Hebrew).

Almog-Bar, M., & Eisenstadt, M. (2015). "You have the feeling that you've run into a wall, and then you have no choice but to set up an association": Characteristics of grassroots organizations in civil society that provide welfare services. *Social Security, 98,* 97–128 (in Hebrew).

Almog-Bar, M., & Greenspan, I. (2019). Civil society organizations in Israel: An up-to-date view based on data from GuideStar-Israel. The Center for the Study of Civil Society and Philanthropy in Israel, at The Hebrew University of Jerusalem (in Hebrew).

Almog-Bar, M., Schmid, H., & Lachman-Lazar, N. (2013). Cross-sectoral partnerships: Theoretical approaches and research findings. The Center for the Study of Civil Society and Philanthropy in Israel, at The Hebrew University of Jerusalem (in Hebrew).

Almog-Bar, M., & Zichlinsky, E. (2010a). "The pin that should annoy the elephant": The interaction between philanthropic foundations and the government in the development of social enterprises. The Center for the Study of Civil Society and Philanthropy in Israel, at The Hebrew University of Jerusalem (in Hebrew).

Almog-Bar, M., & Zichlinsky, E. (2010b). This was supposed to be a partnership: The interaction between philanthropic foundations and the government in the "Yaniv initiative". *Social Security, 83,* 161–194 (in Hebrew).

THE EVOLUTION OF THE ISRAELI THIRD SECTOR   63

Amit, A. (2011). Can two walk together without having met? Planning and implementing mergers of third sector organizations. *Civil Society and the Third sector in Israel,*
3(2), 107–116.

Amit, R., & Kreindler, M. (2010). Management that affects performance improvement
in the third sector: What can be learned from successful managers in the business
sector. *Civil Society and the Third Sector in Israel, 1,* 33–65.

Anheier, H. (2007). Responsibility in the age of globalization. *Civil Society and the Third*
Sector in Israel, 1, 19–38.

Anheier, H. K., Lang, M., & Toepler, S. (2020). Comparative nonprofit sector research:
a critical assessment. In W. W. Powell & P. Bromley (Eds.), *The nonprofit sector: A*
research handbook, 3rd edn (pp. 648–676). Stanford, CA: Stanford University Press.

Auerbach, G. (2008). Local government and the third sector in Israel: Relations between
the Jerusalem municipality and welfare associations. *Social Security, 78,* 11–37.

Auerbach, G. (2009). On philanthropy and effectiveness—the field of education in
Israel. The Center for the Study of Civil Society and Philanthropy in Israel, at The
Hebrew University of Jerusalem (in Hebrew).

Bar, M. (2001). Involvement of voluntary welfare organizations in the processes of
determining welfare policy—the process of determining "disabled child" regulations. *Chevra Ve'Revacha, 2,* 129–158 (in Hebrew).

Bar-Mor, H. (1999). *The third sector: Legal aspects.* Beersheba: Israeli Center for Third
Sector Research, Ben-Gurion University of the Negev (in Hebrew).

Bar-Mor, M., & Iecovich, E. (2007). The relationship between organization formaliza-
tion and awareness of fiduciary duties of board members of nonprofit organization.
Civil Society and the Third Sector in Israel, 1, 7–24.

Belbachin, Y. (2008). *The Ethiopian community in the third sector: Trends in the registra-*
tion of organizations and changes in activity patterns. Beersheba: Israeli Center for
Third Sector Research, Ben-Gurion University of the Negev (in Hebrew).

Ben Eliezer, B. (1999). Is a civil society forming in Israel? Politics and identity in the
new associations. *Israeli Sociology, B*(1), 51–97 (in Hebrew).

Berrebi, C., & Yonah, C. (2017). *Philanthropy in Israel: An updated picture.* Taub Center
for Social Policy Studies in Israel. A Chapter from the State of the Nation Report, 1B,
45–100 (in Hebrew).

Brenner, N., Hazzan, O., Rudich-Choen, A., & Schmid, H. (2010). Survey of philanthropic
foundations and funding bodies in Israel. The Center for the Study of Civil Society
and Philanthropy in Israel, at The Hebrew University of Jerusalem. (Hebrew).

Brochure. (2004). Beersheba: Israeli Center for the Third Sector Research. Ben-Gurion
University of the Negev (in Hebrew).

Brochure. (2007). Beersheba: Israeli Center for the Third Sector Research. Ben-Gurion
University of the Negev (in Hebrew).

Chevra Ve'Revacha (2020). Available at: https://www.gov.il/he/departments/pub lications/reports/molsa-social-and-welfare-magazine.

Defourny, J., & Nyssens, M. (2006). Defining social enterprise. In M. Nyssens (Ed.), *Social enterprise: At the crossroads of market, public policies and civil society* (pp. 3–26). London: Routledge.

Diani, M. (1992). The concept of social movements. *The Sociological Review*, 40(1), 1–25.

Drezner, N. D., Greenspan, I., Katz, H., & Feit, G. (2017). *Philanthropy in Israel: 2016: Patterns of individual giving.* Tel Aviv: Tel Aviv University.

Eran, Y. (1992). *Voluntary organizations in the welfare system.* Tel Aviv: Ramot.

Esping-Andersen, G. (1990). *The three worlds of welfare capitalism.* Cambridge: Polity Press.

Fleischmann, J. L. (2009). Advocacy activities of foundations and their impact on public policy—the American experience. The Center for the Study of Civil Society and Philanthropy in Israel, at The Hebrew University of Jerusalem.

Fogiel-Bijaoui, S. (1998). Women and citizenship in Israel: An analysis of silence. *Politics*, 1, 44–71 (in Hebrew).

Foley, M. W., & Edwards, B. (1996). The paradox of civil society. *Journal of Democracy*, 7(3), 38–52.

Galnoor, I. (2006). *The Committee for examining the roles of the third sector in Israel and the policies adopted towards it: Summary report.* Beersheba: The Israeli Center for Third Sector Research, Ben-Gurion University of the Negev (in Hebrew).

Galnoor, I., Ophir, A., Arnon, A., Bar, M., Gabai, Y., Gidron, B., Zilberstein-Hipsh, S., Katz, O., Liel, R., Limor, N., Mula, W., Machul, A., Armoni, A., Katan, J., Gatas, B., Shiffer, V., & Sharon, E. & Associates. (2003). *The review committee of government policy towards the third sector in Israel.* Beersheba: The Israeli Center for Third Sector Research, Ben-Gurion University of the Negev (in Hebrew).

Gay Israel (2019). *Israel Ministry of Foreign Affairs*, July 18. Available at: https://mfa.gov .il/MFA/IsraelExperience/Pages/Gay_Israel.aspx.

Gidron, B. (1977). Rewards from volunteer work. *Social Security*, 1, 51–63 (in Hebrew).

Gidron, B. (1983). Volunteers satisfaction from their work. *Chevra Ve'Revacha*, 5(3), 259–270 (in Hebrew).

Gidron, B. (1984). Predictors of perseverance and dropout at work among community center volunteers. *Magamot*, 29(2), 180–198 (in Hebrew).

Gidron, B. (1997). The evolution of Israel's third sector: The role of predominant ideology. *Voluntas*, 8(1), 11–38.

Gidron, B. (1999). *Database of the third sector in Israel: Preliminary findings: Registry of associations 1981–1998, government support for third sector organizations 1991–1997.* Beersheba: Israeli Center for Third Sector Research, Ben-Gurion University of the Negev (in Hebrew).

Gidron, B. (2007). Researching the third sector and civil society in Israel: History and current status. *Civil Society and the Third Sector in Israel, 1*, 7–18.

Gidron, B. (2011). Promoting civil society in third sector organizations through participatory management patterns. *Civil Society and the Third Sector in Israel, 3*(2), 29–47.

Gidron, B., & Abbou, I. (2012). *Social enterprises in Israel: Towards a definition*. Kfar Saba: The Israeli Center for the Study of Social Enterprises, Beit Berl College (in Hebrew).

Gidron, B., Abbou, I., Buber-Ben David, N., Greenberg, Y., Givon-Monikendam, Y., Navon, A., & Reuveni, Y. (2017). Social-business enterprises: International comparative research, ICSEM-international comparative social enterprise models. The College of Management, Academic Studies (in Hebrew).

Gidron, B., & Alon, Y. (2004). *Database report of the third sector in Israel 2000. District deployment of the third sector in Israel, wage payments in third sector organizations.* Beersheba: Israeli Center for Third Sector Research, Ben-Gurion University of the Negev (in Hebrew).

Gidron, B., Alon, Y., Schlanger, A., & Schwartz, R. (2006). *The philanthropic funds sector and financing organizations in Israel: Characteristics, roles, relations with the government and ways of conduct.* Beersheba: Israeli Center for Third Sector Research, Ben-Gurion University of the Negev (in Hebrew).

Gidron, B., Bar, M., & Katz, H. (2002). Characteristics of the Israeli organized civil society. *Israeli Sociology, 4*(2), 269–400 (in Hebrew).

Gidron, B., Bar, M., & Katz, H. (2004). *The Israeli third sector.* New York: Kluwer.

Gidron, B., & Bargal, D. (1986). Self-help awareness in Israel: An expression of structural changes and expanding citizen participation. *Nonprofit & Voluntary Sector Quarterly, 15*, 47–56.

Gidron, B., & Chesler, M. (1994). Universal and particular attributes of self-help: A framework for international and intranational analysis. In F. Lavoie, T. Borkman, & B. Gidron (Eds.), *Self-Help and Mutual Aid Groups* (pp. 1–44). New York: The Haworth Press.

Gidron, B., & Katz, H. (1998). *The third sector in Israel. First analysis: boundaries, characters and processes.* Beersheba: Israeli Center for Third Sector Research, Ben-Gurion University of the Negev (in Hebrew).

Gidron, B., & Katz, H. (1999). *The third sector in Israel: Economic data.* Beersheba: Israeli Center for Third Sector Research, Ben-Gurion University of the Negev (in Hebrew).

Gidron, B., & Katz, H. (2001). Patterns of government funding to third sector organizations as reflecting de facto policy and their implications on the structure of the sector in Israel. *International Journal of Public Administration, 24*(11), 1133–1159. Israeli Center for Third Sector Research, Ben-Gurion University of the Negev.

Gidron, B., Katz, H., & Bar, M. (2000). *The third sector in Israel 2000: Roles of the sector.* Beersheba: Israeli Center for Third Sector Research, Ben-Gurion University of the Negev (in Hebrew).

Gidron, B., Katz, H., Bar-Mor, H., Katan, Y., Silber, I., & Telias, M. (2003). Through a new lens: The third sector and Israeli society, *Israel Studies, 8*(1), 20–59.

Gidron, B., Katz, H., & Bar, M. (2003). *The third sector in Israel: Between welfare state and civil society.* Tel Aviv: Hakibbutz Hameuchad, Red Line Series (in Hebrew).

Gidron, B., Katz, S., & Hasenfeld, Y. (2002). *Mobilizing for peace.* New York: Oxford University Press.

Gidron, B., & Lazar, A. (1998). Level religiosity and patterns of giving and volunteering in the Israeli public. *Social Security, 51,* 44–56 (in Hebrew).

Gidron, B., Schlanger, A., & Alon, Y. (2008). The contribution of foreign philanthropic foundations to Israeli society. *Civil Society and the Third Sector in Israel, 2*(1), 33–50.

Greenspan, I. (2014). Environmental philanthropy: The relationship between philanthropic funds and environmental organizations in Israel. The Center for the Study of Civil Society and Philanthropy in Israel, at The Hebrew University of Jerusalem.

Haaretz (2019). The Berl Kenzelson Foundation's hate report reveals: haters, especially Arabs and ultra-orthodox. August 11. Available at: https://www.haaretz.co.il/captain/net/1.7657735.

Haber, K. (2011). The "managed giving" ethos in the field of Israeli International humanitarian aid. *Civil Society and the Third Sector in Israel, 3*(2), 49–85.

Haski-Leventhal, D., & Kabalo, P. (2009). From the well-known Hanadiv to the New Israel Fund: Donation channels to Eretz Israel and the State of Israel from the end of the Ottoman period to the present day. The Center for the Study of Civil Society and Philanthropy in Israel, at The Hebrew University of Jerusalem.

Haski-Leventhal, D., Yogev-Keren, H., & Katz, H. (2011). *Philanthropy in Israel 2008: Patterns of volunteering, giving and organ donations.* Beersheba: Israeli Center for Third Sector Research, Ben-Gurion University of the Negev.

Hazan, O. (2009). The relationship between government funding and private funding of the third sector funding. The Center for the Study of Civil Society and Philanthropy in Israel, at The Hebrew University of Jerusalem.

Hazan, O. (2010). On donations, tax benefits and everything in between: Individual and corporate donations to non-profits, and the impact of tax policy on these donations. The Center for the Study of Civil Society and the Philanthropy in Israel, at The Hebrew University of Jerusalem.

Himeyn Raisch, N. (2008). Women and civil society in Israel. The Israel Democracy Institute Press. Available at: https://en.idi.org.il/articles/6749.

Iekowitz, A. (2006). Public managements in voluntary organizations: Who they represent and how they are elected. *Chevra Ve'Revacha, 26*(1), 87–109 (in Hebrew).

Iekowitz, A., & Katan, Y. (2005). Unique characteristics of voluntary organizations—do they exist in non-profit organizations for the elderly? *Social Security, 70,* 138–158 (in Hebrew).

Iekowitz, A., Naftali, M., Gidron, B., & Bar-Mor, H. (2002). *Public managements of third sector organizations in Israel: Characteristics and structural aspects, functions and organizations.* Beersheba: Israeli Center for Third Sector Research, Ben-Gurion University of the Negev.

Israel NPOS Yearbook (2020). Ministry of Justice-Corporate Authority-Registrar of Associations-GuideStar, Joint Alka, and Institute of Law and Philanthropy, The Buchman Faculty of Law, Tel Aviv University. Available at: https://www.guidestar .org.il/home.

Israel Prime Minister's Office (2006). *The inter-ministerial review committee of government support to third sector organizations.* Jerusalem: Prime Minister's Office (in Hebrew).

Israel Prime Minister's Office (2008). Government of Israel, civil society, and the business community: Partnership, empowerment, and transparency. Policy document, Jerusalem (in Hebrew).

Israel's Independence Day 2019 (PDF report). Israel Central Bureau of Statistics. 6 May. Available at: https://www.cbs.gov.il/en/mediarelease/Pages/2019/Israel-Inde pendence-Day-2019.aspx.

Israeli Sociology (2020). About us. Available at: https://socis.tau.ac.il/index.php/en/ about-us.

Jaffe, E. D. (1979). Non-conventional philanthropy. *Moment Magazine, 5*(5), 63–64.

Jaffe, E. D. (1982). *Giving wisely: The Israel guide to volunteer and nonprofit social services.* Jerusalem: Koren Publishers.

Jaffe, E. D. (1983). *Claim and protest: Future Prediction of voluntary organizations in Israel.* Jerusalem: American Jewish Committee (in Hebrew).

Jaffe, E. D. (1985). *Givers and spenders: The politics of charity in Israel.* Jerusalem: Ariel Publishers.

Jaffe, E. D. (1987). The crisis in Jewish philanthropy. *Tikkun Magazine, 2*(4), 27–31.

Jaffe, E. D., York, A., & Kfir, A. (2011). Personal characteristics distinguishing direct volunteers from board members of voluntary organizations. *Civil Society and the Third Sector in Israel, 3*(2), 87–105.

Jamal, A. (2017). *Arab civil society in Israel: New elites, social capital and challenging power structures.* Bnei Brak: Hakibbutz Hameuchad.

Jamal, A., Almog-Bar, M., Kokbin, V., & Eseed, R. (2019). Arab-Palestinians in Israel civil society. The Center for the Study of Civil Society and Philanthropy in Israel, at The Hebrew University of Jerusalem and The Walter Lebach Institute for Jewish-Arab Coexistence through Education, at Tel Aviv University.

James, E. (1987). The nonprofit sector in comparative perspective. In W. W. Powell (Ed.), *The nonprofit sector: A research handbook* (pp. 397–415). New Haven, CT: Yale University Press.

Kabalo, P. (2009). A fifth nonprofit regime? Revisiting social origins theory using Jewish associational life as a new state model. *Nonprofit and Voluntary Sector Quarterly, 38*(4), 627–642.

Katan, Y. (1988). Voluntary organizations: Substitute or partner of the state in a welfare field. *Social Security, 32,* 57–73 (in Hebrew).

Katan, Y. (2007). *Privatization in the personal social services in Israel.* Jerusalem: Ministry of Welfare and Social Services (in Hebrew).

Katz, H., Alon, Y. Gidron, B., & Babis, D. (2006). *Data on the third sector in Israel, 2006: Status of the third sector in Israel organizations in the status of a public institution for the purpose of donations.* Beersheba: Israeli Center for Third Sector Research, Ben-Gurion University of the Negev.

Katz, H., Alon, Y., Gidron, B., Yogev, H., Yakobi, M., Levinsson, E., & Raviv, E. (2007). The Israeli third sector during the Lebanon War (summer 2006): Its functioning and its roles during a state of emergency. *Civil Society and the Third Sector in Israel, 1,* 39–64.

Katz, H., Gidron, B., & Limor, N. (2009). *The third sector in Israel—its character and structure and the policy towards it.* Beersheba: The Israeli Center for Third Sector Research, Ben-Gurion University (in Hebrew).

Katz, H., & Greenspan, I. (2015). Giving in Israel: From old traditions to an emerging culture of philanthropy? In P. Wiepking and F. Handy (Eds.), *The Palgrave handbook of global philanthropy,* pp. 316–337. Basingstoke: Palgrave Macmillan.

Katz, H., & Haski-Leventhal. (2008). Does faith lead to charity? Disentangling the effect of religiosity on philanthropy. *Civil Society and the Third Sector in Israel, 2*(1), 51–72.

Katz, H., Levinson, E., & Gidron, B. (2007). *Philanthropy in Israel 2006: Patterns of giving and volunteering of the Israeli public.* Beersheba: Israeli Center for Third Sector Research, Ben-Gurion University of the Negev.

Katz, H., & Yogev, H. (2010). *Israel's third sector in the financial crisis: Can we do more with less?* Beersheba: Ben-Gurion University, Israeli Center for Third-sector Research (in Hebrew).

Katz, H., & Yogev-Keren, H. (2013). *The labor market of the third sector in Israel: Data and trends 2000–2009.* Beersheba: The Israeli Center for Third Sector Research, Ben-Gurion University of the Negev (in Hebrew).

Kaufman, R., & Gidron, B. (2006). *Institutionalization and specialization of protest? Characteristics and trends in the establishment of organizations for social change in Israel.* Beersheba: The Israeli Center for Third Sector Research, Ben-Gurion University (in Hebrew).

Kogot, T., & Ritov, I. (2010). Psychological effects on the motivation for philanthropic activity: The effect of the victim identified on its origins and boundaries. The Center for the Study of Civil Society and Philanthropy in Israel, at The Hebrew University of Jerusalem.

Kramer, R. M. (1970). *Community development in Israel and the Netherlands: A comparative analysis.* Berkeley: Institute of International Studies, University of California.

Kramer, R. M. (1976). *The voluntary service agency in Israel.* Berkeley: Institute of International Studies, University of California.

Kramer, R. M. (1981). *Voluntary agencies in welfare state.* Berkeley: University of California Press.

Kramer, R. M. (1984). Voluntary agencies and social change in Israel, 1972–1982. *Israel Social Science Research, 2*(2), 55–72.

Lazar, H. (2013). Philanthropic relationships from the perspective of the recipients: The case of social change organizations in Israel. The Center for the Study of Civil Society and Philanthropy in Israel, at The Hebrew University of Jerusalem.

Levi D'Ancona, L. (2010). Explorations in contemporary European Jewish philanthropy: The Italian case in context. The Center for the Study of Civil Society and Philanthropy in Israel, at The Hebrew University of Jerusalem.

Limor, N. (2004). Examination of the third sector in Israel (Report). Jerusalem.

Limor, N. (2008). The unreachable jars of honey. *Civil Society and the Third Sector in Israel, 2*(1), 95–136.

Limor, N. (2010). Civil society and the third sector in Israel (Report). The Israel Democracy Institute (IDI).

Limor, N., & Avishai, L. (2013). *Together-constructing government-civil society organizations partnerships.* Jerusalem: The Van Leer Jerusalem Institute.

Lior, I. (2015). Israel actually ranks low in tolerance of LGBT people, survey says. *Haaretz*, August 23.

Livnat, I., & Almog-Bar, M. (2018). "Lots of freedom, but also lots of mess and lots of lack of knowledge". The employment experience of middle managers in third sector organizations in Israel. *Chevra Ve'Revacha, 38*, 67–96 (in Hebrew).

Madhala, S., Almog-Bar, M., & Gal, J. (2018). Israeli welfare organizations: A snapshot. The Center for the Study of Civil Society and Philanthropy in Israel, at The Hebrew University of Jerusalem.

Malach, G., & Cahaner, L. (2018). *Statistical report on ultra-orthodox (Haredi) society in Israel, 2018.* The Israel Democracy Institute.

Mano, R. (2010). Organizational crisis, adaptation, and innovation in Israel's nonprofit organizations: A learning approach. *Administration in Social Work, 4*(34), 344–350.

Menuchin, I. (2011). Basic principles of civil society. *Civil Society and the Third Sector in Israel, 3*(2), 7–28.

Meslin, M. E., Rooney, M. P., & Wolf, G. J. (2008). Health-related philanthropy: Toward understanding the relationship between the donation of the body (and its parts) and traditional forms of philanthropic giving. *Civil Society and the Third Sector in Israel, 2*(1), 73–94.

Minkoff, D. C. (1997). Producing social capital. *American Behavioral Scientist, 40*(5), 606–619.

Neu, P. (1993). Needs assessment of Arab-Israeli non-governmental organizations for inter-agency support mechanism. The Galilee Society for Health Research and the Services (unpublished).

Portugaly, A., & Miller-Danieli, N. (2007). Earned revenue in nonprofit organizations: The realization of social mission through commercial ventures. *Civil Society and the Third Sector in Israel, 1*, 25–49.

Raichel, A., Gidron, B., & Shani-Gamliel, N. (2000). *Social responsibility of business in Israel.* Beersheba: Israeli Center for Third Sector Research, Ben-Gurion University of the Negev (in Hebrew).

Rikoula, R., Mano, S., & Hareven, L. (2007). Strategic choices of survival in social organizations: Accountability and change as reactions to environmental influence. *Civil Society and the Third Sector in Israel, 1*, 51–74.

Rosolio, D. (2006). The third sector and civil society, an analytic approach. *Israeli Sociology, 7*(2), 425–430 (in Hebrew).

Rozenhek, Z., & Silber, I. (2000). *The historical development of the Israeli third sector.* Beersheba: Israeli Center for Third-sector Research, Ben-Gurion University of the Negev.

Rudich, A. (2007). Not just human love—philanthropy in the light of theory and research. The Center for the Study of Civil Society and Philanthropy in Israel, at The Hebrew University of Jerusalem.

Salamon, J. (2008). *Jewish funds.* Jerusalem: The Center for the Study of Civil Society and Philanthropy in Israel, at The Hebrew University of Jerusalem.

Salamon, L. M., & Anheier, H. K. (1998). Social origins of civil society: Explaining the non-profit sector cross-nationally, *Voluntas, 9*, 213–248.

Salamon, L. M., Anheier, H. K., List, R., Toepler, S., Sokolowsky, S. W., & Associates (1999). *Global civil society: Dimensions of the nonprofit sector.* Baltimore, MD: The Johns Hopkins University Institute for Policy Studies.

Schmid, H. (2011). Characteristics of Israeli philanthropy in the 21st century: Motives and barriers for giving and future developments. The Center for the Study of Civil Society and Philanthropy in Israel, at The Hebrew University of Jerusalem.

Schmid, H. (2013). The impact of the various sources of funding on the organizational, strategic, financial and managerial behavior of non-profit human services organizations. The Center for the Study of Civil Society and Philanthropy in Israel, at The Hebrew University of Jerusalem.

Schmid, H. (2015). Civil society in Israel: Changes, trends and direction of action for the future. *Social Security, 98*, 5–14 (in Hebrew).

Schmid, H., & Almog-Bar, M. (2013). Cross-sectoral partnerships: Research findings, conclusions and implications for the practice of partnerships. The Center for the Study of Civil Society and Philanthropy in Israel, at The Hebrew University of Jerusalem.

Schmid, H. & Almog-Bar, M. (2016). Intersectoral partnerships in Israel: Inputs, processes and products. The Center for the Study of Civil Society and Philanthropy in Israel, at The Hebrew University of Jerusalem.

Schmid, H., Almog-Bar, M., & Niral, R. (2008). Political advocacy activities of non-profit organizations providing social services. *Social Security, 78*, 11–37 (in Hebrew).

Schmid, H., & Rudich, A. (2008). A survey of the general public's attitudes towards philanthropy and philanthropists. The Center for the Study of Civil Society and Philanthropy in Israel, at The Hebrew University of Jerusalem.

Schmid, H., & Rudich-Cohn, A. (2012). Elite philanthropy in Israel. *Society, 49*(2), 175–181.

Schmid, H., Rudich, A., & Shaul Bar-Nisisim, H. (2009). Elite philanthropy in Israel: Characteristics, motivations and donation patterns. The Center for the Study of Civil Society and Philanthropy in Israel, at The Hebrew University of Jerusalem.

Schmid, H., & Shaul Bar-Nisisim, H. (2013). The globalization of philanthropy: Means, channels and giving of diasporas. The Center for the Study of Civil Society and Philanthropy in Israel, at The Hebrew University of Jerusalem.

Schmid, H., & Shaul Bar-Nisisim, H. (2015a). "Can the two go together?": Government and philanthropy relationship in Israel, situation and thinking for the future. The Center for the Study of Civil Society and the Philanthropy in Israel, at The Hebrew University of Jerusalem.

Schmid, H., & Shaul Bar-Nisisim, H. (2015b). "Can the two go together?": Government and philanthropy relationship in Israel, situation and thinking for the future. *Social Security, 98*, 63–95 (in Hebrew).

Schmid, H., Shaul Bar-Nisisim, H., & Niral, R. (2018). Intergenerational transmission of philanthropic behavior among wealthy donor families in Israel. The Center for the Study of Civil Society and Philanthropy in Israel, at The Hebrew University of Jerusalem.

Schneider, A., & Shoham, L. (2017). Arab philanthropy in Israel. Insight into strategic giving. Inter-Agency Task Force on Israeli Arab Issues.

Schusterman, S. (2010). Topography of self-help groups in Jerusalem. *Civil Society and the Third Sector in Israel, 1*, 67–81.

Schwartz, E. (2009). The implications of the economic crisis on the third sector. The Knesset Research and Information Center.

Sembira, G. (2008). A clear plan will illuminate your idea? The decision-making process for establishing a family foundation: A case analysis. *Civil Society and the Third Sector in Israel, 2*(1),137–159.

Sembira, G., & Fuchs, E. (2007). Social networks and civil society. *Civil Society and the Third Sector in Israel, 1*, 97–102.

Senor, D., & Singer, S. (2009). *Startup nation: The story of Israel's economic miracle.* New York: Twelve.

Sharir, M., Heilborn, S., & Lazar, A. (2005). *Civil society and local government—civil society organizations in Rishon Lezion and the local authority's treatment of them in 2000–2002.* Beersheba: Israeli Center for Third Sector Research, Ben-Gurion University of the Negev (in Hebrew).

Shay, S., Lazar, A., Duchin, R., & Gidron, B. (1999). *Philanthropy in Israel. Patterns of public donation and volunteering—research report.* Beersheba: Israeli Center for Third Sector Research, Ben-Gurion University of the Negev (in Hebrew).

Shimoni, B. (2008). Businesses and new philanthropy in Israel: Ethnography of major donors. The Center for the Study of Civil Society and Philanthropy in Israel, at The Hebrew University of Jerusalem.

Silber, I. (2008). *The philanthropic era? The Israeli case.* Beersheba: Israel Center for Third Sector Research, Ben-Gurion University of the Negev. (in Hebrew).

Silber, I., & Rosenhek, Z. (2000). *Historical development of the nonprofit sector in Israel.* Beersheba: Israel Center for Third Sector Research, Ben-Gurion University of the Negev.

Solek, M. (2010). The meaning of philanthropy. *Civil Society and the Third Sector in Israel, 1*, 83–104.

Strychman, N., & Marshud, F. (2007). Adaptation in a period of growth: Israeli nonprofit organizations for social change. *Civil Society and the Third Sector in Israel, 1*, 65–103.

Tamir, I. (2007). Three-sectoral local partnerships: Another way to strengthen the community and the settlement. *Civil Society and the Third Sector in Israel, 1*, 107–110.

Telias, M., Katan, J., & Gidron, B. (2000). *The government and the local authority policy towards the third sector in Israel.* Beersheba: Israeli Center for Third Sector Research, Ben-Gurion University of the Negev (in Hebrew).

The Association for Civil Rights in Israel (2014). Available at: https://law.acri.org.il/he/30852.

The Interface Round Table Staff (2010). From the field: To establish a dialogue between sectors in Israel—the round table interfaces—the first year. *Civil Society and the Third Sector in Israel, 1*, 105–113.

The National Insurance Institute (2020). Publications, journals. Available at: https://www.btl.gov.il/Publications/Social_Security/Pages/default.aspx.

The Round Table in the Prime Minister's Office (2020). Available at: http://beinmigzari.pmo.gov.il/PMO-RoundTable/Pages/default.aspx.

Van Leer Institute (2020). Available at: https://www.vanleer.org.il/.

Weinheber, B. C. (2011). *The round-table: A national framework for inter-sectoral discourse.* Jerusalem: Prime Minister's Office (in Hebrew).

Weinheber, B. C., Sembira, G., & Oz-Ari, M. (2015). *Civil society programs in the education system. Joint regularization test case: The tri-sector round-table.* Jerusalem: Ministry of Education (in Hebrew).

Yanay-Ventura, G., & Livena, T. (2010). Effective volunteer management—the point of view of managers. *Social Security, 84,* 129–157 (in Hebrew).

Yishai, Y. (1987). *Interest groups in Israel.* Tel Aviv: Am-Oved (in Hebrew).

Yishai, Y. (1998). Civil society in transition: Interest politics in Israel. *Annals of the American Academy of Political and Social Science, 555*(1), 147–162.

Yishai, Y. (2003). *Between recruitment and reconciliation: Civil society in Israel.* Jerusalem: Carmel Press (in Hebrew).

Young, D. R., & Casey, J. (2017). Supplementary, complementary or adversarial? Nonprofit—government relations. In E. T. Boris & C. E. Steuerle (Eds.), *Nonprofits and government: Collaboration and conflict,* 3rd edn (pp. 37–70). Lanham, MD: Rowman & Littlefield.

Zeidan, E. (2005). *Volunteering, donations, and attitudes toward organizations in the Arab-Palestinian community in Israel: Reconsideration.* Beersheba: Israeli Center for Third Sector Research, Ben-Gurion University of the Negev.

Zeidan, E., & Ghanem, A. (2000). *Donation and volunteering in the Arab-Palestinian community in Israel.* Beersheba: Israeli Center for Third Sector Research, Ben-Gurion University of the Negev.

Zichlinsky, E. (2010). The impact of the processes of partial privatization and commercialization on the characteristics of third sector organizations in Israel. *Social Security, 82,* 129–157.

Printed in the United States
By Bookmasters